South London

Edited by Steve Twelvetree

YoungWriters
First published in Great Britain in 2005 by:
Young Writers
Remus House
Coltsfoot Drive
Peterborough
PE2 9JX
Telephone: 01733 890066
Website: www.youngwriters.co.uk

SB ISBN 1 84602 148 0

Foreword

Young Writers was established in 1991 and has been passionately devoted to the promotion of reading and writing in children and young adults ever since. The quest continues today. Young Writers remains as committed to the fostering of burgeoning poetic and literary talent as ever.

This year's Young Writers competition has proven as vibrant and dynamic as ever and we are delighted to present a showcase of the best poetry from across the UK. Each poem has been carefully selected from a wealth of *Playground Poets* entries before ultimately being published in this, our thirteenth primary school poetry series.

Once again, we have been supremely impressed by the overall high quality of the entries we have received. The imagination, energy and creativity which has gone into each young writer's entry made choosing the best poems a challenging and often difficult but ultimately hugely rewarding task - the general high standard of the work submitted amply vindicating this opportunity to bring their poetry to a larger appreciative audience.

We sincerely hope you are pleased with our final selection and that you will enjoy *Playground Poets South London* for many years to come.

Elephant

This is an ugly thing,
That smells like what you put in a bin,
Stomping hard, stomping strong,
Stomping harder than King Kong.

Flapping ears, flapping tail,
Never slivers like a snail,
Long thick trunk swaying too,
Bumping animals like a kangaroo.

Ardit Mustafa (10)
Allen Edwards Primary School, Stockwell

The Magnificent Jeep

The magnificent jeep.
My jeep is racing-red.
Like a red, new, crystal Ferrari.
Its wheels are like a shiny spinning top.
Its doors are like spaceship doors opening.
Its underneath is like glowing neon lights.
I will never crash when I'm in this car.

Reece Green (9)
Allen Edwards Primary School, Stockwell

The Sun

The sun is a light bulb, that lightens up the sky,
The sun is a balloon, that floats above us,
It is a star, that shines on top of the world,
It is a bowling ball, that rolls around the Earth,
It is a torch, that flashes on us.
The sun.

Rachael Ogunniyi (10)
Allen Edwards Primary School, Stockwell

Parrot

Why do you repeat what I say?
Repeat what I say.
Can you stop repeating me?
Repeating me.
Be quiet you blue and orange bird.
I heard, I heard.

Try being quiet for half an hour.
Half an hour.
Yeah start from now.
Start from now.
I think you chat a lot.
Fetch a pot, fetch a pot.

Hold on a minute I think you're lying to me.
Lying to you, me.
I caught you red-handed.
Red-footed, beaked, handed.
Just you wait.
What if I'm late?

Parrot.
Parrot ha, ha, ha.

Marissa Clarke-Ryder (9)
Allen Edwards Primary School, Stockwell

The Rain

The rain is a mirror on the ground,
The rain is a teardrop dropping from the sky,
The rain is a shower bathing poor people,
The rain is a drink filling your cup every time,
The rain is a pool that people cry in
The rain is a river flowing to the sea,
The rain is a reflection when you look in the mirror.

Karl Alexis (10)
Allen Edwards Primary School, Stockwell

Excuses

(Based on 'Excuses' by Allan Ahlberg)

'Oh George where is your homework?'
'Er, dog ate it Miss.'
'Is that your excuse George?'
Teacher said with a hiss.

'So are you doing PE today?'
'Er, broke my arm Miss.'
'Why isn't there a plaster on it?'
Teacher said with a hiss.

'I'm sending a letter to your mum.'
'Please don't do that Miss.'
'Tell me why I shouldn't?'
Teacher said with a hiss.

'She'll smack my bum
And I won't be able to sit down Miss.'
'Well that'll be fun!'
Teacher said with a hiss.

George Issom (10)
Allen Edwards Primary School, Stockwell

The Rain

The rain is a mirror dropping on the ground,
The rain is a teardrop crying for help,
The rain is a shower having a second bath,
The rain is a pool that people cry in,
The rain is a river flowing to the Earth,
The rain is a river flowing to the ground,
The rain is a drink filling up your cup,
The rain is a puddle that once was clean but now it's dirty,
The rain is a sea that people swim through.

Andrea Charlton (10)
Allen Edwards Primary School, Stockwell

Weights

I put some weights,
On my body and head,
Put a chair on top,
Then feigned to be dead.

Mum came in
And told me to move,
So I put on some music
And started to groove.

While I was moving
I stepped on a weight,
'Ouch, ouch, ouch!'
I boiled with hate.

Jeziah Rodney (10)
Allen Edwards Primary School, Stockwell

The Sun

The sun is a sizzling pan that sizzles all around the world,
The sun is a torch shining on people,
The sun is a bouncing ball, rising and falling,
It is a light bulb shining in the bright sky,
It is a balloon floating in the blue.

Amy Meite (9)
Allen Edwards Primary School, Stockwell

Space

Dark and silent
Freezing, beautiful and scary.
Stars are flying by the planets.
Wonderful.

Joey Cassidy (10)
Allen Edwards Primary School, Stockwell

Playground

Everyone playing happily,
No one in the corner sitting sadly,
The children are fair,
Everyone laughs and shares.

There's a lot of laughter,
When you chase after your peers
Some children walking and talking,
Others running and skipping.

So everyone loves the playground
And always is fair and share,
The playground is a good place to be,
So don't be rude and always respect he and she.

Topaz Wisdom (9)
Allen Edwards Primary School, Stockwell

Love

Love is as red as your heart,
It tastes like a sweet strawberry,
It smells like a bunch of flowers,
It looks like a rainbow,
It sounds like bells ringing,
It feels like being on a beach.

Patricia Marques (10)
Allen Edwards Primary School, Stockwell

Kennings

Face smiler
Hot shiner
Fire breather
Skin changer
Fashion maker.

Kawtar Serroukh (10)
Allen Edwards Primary School, Stockwell

Hearts

Love is forever,
Nothing can be better,
Roses on the bed,
I'm in love with Ed,
I fancy him so,
My heart is so low,
When without him,
His girlfriend is Kim,
My life is so dim,
When without him.

Shalini Bayliss-Friend (10)
Allen Edwards Primary School, Stockwell

Golden

You can dream of gold,
You can have a golden egg,
It can be crinkly, shiny, glittery,
Or maybe beautiful instead.
The colour of a real yolk is gold,
Gold, gold, gold.

Maleika Coker-Harewood (11)
Allen Edwards Primary School, Stockwell

Love

Love is pink like blossoms.
It tastes like suckleberry strawberries with cream on top.
It smells like the aroma of sweet perfume.
It looks like hearts surrounding your true love.
It sounds like ringing bells.
It feels like you have been shot by Cupid.

Charlotte Obadiaru (11)
Allen Edwards Primary School, Stockwell

Youngsters

Graffiti is what youngsters do,
Simple, as I don't have a clue,
They might do their tags or other called names,
They might do bad stuff what they call games,
They get all the latest clothes and spend all their money,
They happy-slap people which they think is funny,
All they do is stay in and play PlayStation,
They go to find a job with no education.

Marcus Palmer (11)
Allen Edwards Primary School, Stockwell

The Street's Noise

Loud and different every day.
Children screaming, going out to play.
Always happy in the streets.
Sixteen-year-olds making up beats.
Always excited but stay on their feet
Friends forever, always together
Making up raps to forget about the weather.

Magno Neto (11)
Allen Edwards Primary School, Stockwell

Anger

Anger is black clouds.
It tastes like milk that has gone off.
It smells like rotten cheese.
It looks like blazing fire.
It sounds like an explosion.
It feels like you have got constipation!

Petra Henry (10)
Allen Edwards Primary School, Stockwell

Anger

Anger is as black as a dark cloud.
It tastes like a rotten apple.
Anger smells like a garbage disposal.
It looks like a big pile of rubbish.
Anger sounds like a loud explosion.
It feels like your legs are going to fall off.

Kirk Wisdom (10)
Allen Edwards Primary School, Stockwell

Jaguar

Fast runner
Spotted dasher
Long tailed killer
Deer hunter
Meat eater.

Jacob Trenoweth (10)
Allen Edwards Primary School, Stockwell

Michael Jackson

Michael Jackson is the best
We all know he's better than the rest
Does the moonwalk upside down
Never ever has to frown
Has a theme park in Las Vegas
We all know he's mega famous
Faces allegations in court
That's why we have to give him full support.

Kevin Kasozi (10)
Clapham Manor Primary School, Clapham

A Poem About Anger

The colour is red like blood dripping down my forehead.
It sounds like a building is going to explode.
It tastes like hot burning pepper.
It smells like fire and flame.
It looks like the sun is going to blow.
It feels like a bomb is shaking.
It reminds me of me beating up my cousin!

Carl Fordjuor (7)
Clapham Manor Primary School, Clapham

Legend Of Zelda: Minish Cap

Brave sword slashing
Link is bashing
Monsters crashing
To the ground
Earth, fire element found!
Power up your sword
With that strange buzzing sound
Ezlo's looking round and round.

Hani Malcolm Ibrahim (9)
Clapham Manor Primary School, Clapham

A Poem About Anger

It is red.
It sounds like a volcano rumbling.
It tastes like a fireball.
It smells like an oven exploding everywhere.
What does it look like? It looks like a bull charging.
What does it feel like? It feels like coal burning.
It reminds me of when I watched a volcano show.

Harvey Wilson (7)
Clapham Manor Primary School, Clapham

My Squirrel Snow-shaker

Snowflakes are floating in the air;
Magical wind is flowing,
Nothing can harm me with this in my palm
The water is always flowing.

My snow-shaker makes no sound
Nothing keeps us apart,
Squirrels and glitter are the magic for me,
I don't need to train them, they're smart.

Brown, red and white
Is the colour of my magical friend,
I play with her all night and day
If they go, my broken heart will never mend.

The markings for me
Are right there in sight
She's such a good guard dog
All day and night.

Ffion Jones (10)
Clapham Manor Primary School, Clapham

Laughter

Laughter is clear like the windowpane.
It sounds as if I were a clown who put balls down his trousers and started giggling.
It smells like laughing bubbles popping.
It feels like you are being lifted up by laughing gas.
It tastes as if you were swallowing something nasty.
Laugher reminds me of one day when I was playing around.

Miya Bailey (8)
Clapham Manor Primary School, Clapham

Reflecting At Wet Play

I look out the window,
But my life just bounces back at me.
When I want to run away,
My life just catches up with me.

Sometimes I wish,
I can close my eyes and disappear.
But when I open them,
I happen to reappear.

I feel like I'm locked out,
From a good life and good feeling.
But yet I don't understand,
What a good life is with human beings.

Look at me, where am I?
I can't see myself in the mirror,
But when I can see myself,
It just makes me shiver!

I look out the window,
But my life just bounces back at me.
When I want to run away,
My life just catches up with me!

Josephine Grindley (10)
Clapham Manor Primary School, Clapham

A Poem About Anger

Anger is red like the blazing sun.
It sounds like bursting lava.
It tastes like firewood.
It smells like shooting fireworks.
It looks like floating sparks in the air.
It feels like burning light.
It reminds me of sparks and light.

Jahmael Birmingham (7)
Clapham Manor Primary School, Clapham

I Love Football

I love football
It's the best thing to do
When you do it you
Will cheer with joy.

I love football
When you kick the ball
And then when you do a back kick
You will be on the floor.

I love football
Curl it like
David Beckham
And kick it all the way to Peckham
I love football it's so great!

Shaqkiel-Henry Jackson (9)
Clapham Manor Primary School, Clapham

The Playground

Children clapping
Nursery slapping
Kids rapping
Basketball slamming
Kids crying
Others sighing
Tennis throwing
This girl is sewing
Sinks flooding
Teachers nodding
Juniors running
His reading is stunning
I'm learning
He's moaning.

Craig Barnaby (11)
Clapham Manor Primary School, Clapham

The Playground

Football shooting
Whistle tooting
Hands clapping
Children singing
Tale telling
Toilets smelling
Cool running
Water fountains
Children fighting
Fist crunching
Trees rustling
Up and down
Running races
There and back
Basketballs popping
Sounding like popcorn
Line forming
Children screaming
Adrenalin rushing
Around and around.

Chloe Clynshaw (11)
Clapham Manor Primary School, Clapham

Why Am I Left Out?

Why am I left out?
It's so boring being here.
Why am I left out?
Sitting on this crusty chair
Why am I left out?
Just me, what can I do?
Why am I left out?
What if it was you?

Charley Sestanovich (9)
Clapham Manor Primary School, Clapham

A Poem About Fun

Fun is multicoloured like children playing in the playground.
It sounds like people on a roller coaster screaming really loud.
It tastes like chewy, sticky, yummy sweets.
It smells like candy just coming out from the machine.
It looks like a wonderful drawing of an artist's best painting.
It feels like a fluffy cat eating up all his food.
It reminds me of me at Chessington World of Adventure in
Bubble Works.

Tomomi Kishimoto-Eley (7)
Clapham Manor Primary School, Clapham

Silence

Silence is turquoise.
Like a dark, dark, cold room that's been standing for
hundreds of years.
It smells as damp as if an elephant has just sprayed water
on the ceiling.
It feels like all your friends have left you alone.
It tastes sad and bitter like a lemon.
Silence reminds me of when someone has been abandoned
in a small box.

Ella Ferron (9)
Clapham Manor Primary School, Clapham

Laughter

Laughter is yellow like the sun beaming down one of its beams.
It sounds like one billion balls bouncing madly in your tummy.
It smells like fried chicken about to be taken out of the oven.
It feels like my head may explode at any moment.
It tastes like a sweet being boiled.
Laughter reminds me of people enjoying themselves at a party.

Ephraim Kihondo (9)
Clapham Manor Primary School, Clapham

Silence

Silence is white,
Like a piece of paper with not a thing on it even a spot of ink.
It sounds like a world without sounds or voices
Like when you go to bed, the noise of not a single argument.
It smells like air swooshing about but without the noise,
Like when the spray has lost its smell.
It feels like getting swallowed into darkness
Where nobody dares to visit.
It tastes like a drop of rain on your tongue
That can dissolve so quickly you don't even feel it.
Silence reminds me of being in a world of nothingness
even with no air.

Amarachi Anosike (9)
Clapham Manor Primary School, Clapham

Anger

Anger is red like blood dripping from a vampire's mouth.
It sounds like someone screaming in the air.
It smells like dry flesh in rotting mud.
It feels like the Devil pulling your heart from your belly.
It tastes like dry skin being peeled off.
It reminds me of being in Hell.

Gael Benjamin (8)
Clapham Manor Primary School, Clapham

Laughter

Laughter is like the yellow sunshine that is hot, hot, hot!
It sounds like children laughing about the clown.
It smells like perfume spreading around the world of laughter.
It feels like balloons exploding in your belly.
It tastes like sweets that make you laugh.
Laugher reminds me of my friends laughing.

Maira Dibao (8)
Clapham Manor Primary School, Clapham

Silence

Silence is a very light blue like the sea near the beach.
Silence sounds like people speaking in their own heads.
Silence smells like a gust of dust making you sneeze right out
of your nose.
Silence feels like no vibration on the new and improved carpet
That makes you shiver like a rattlesnake's tail.
Silence tastes like one piece of sugar on your breakfast.
Silence reminds me of peaceful things in my head
To make me relax on my cosy sofa in my bedroom.

Atlanta D'Archambaud (8)
Clapham Manor Primary School, Clapham

Laughter

Laughter is yellow like the sun shining on me.
It sounds like somebody singing like they're at a parade.
It smells like McDonalds wafting across my nose.
It feels like a soft feather going near my face.
It tastes like honey on toast trickling down my chin.
It reminds me of when I went to Birmingham and played
with my cousins.

Lashay Preddie (9)
Clapham Manor Primary School, Clapham

Silence

Silence is black like the cold misty day.
It sounds like a newborn baby ant taking its first breath.
It smells like the dust a rabbit leaves behind when it leaps.
It tastes like a sour lemon.
It feels like me being left behind in the dark.
It reminds me of loneliness.

Sammy Afewerki (8)
Clapham Manor Primary School, Clapham

Black Dragon

Silent silk, slick in the shiny night
As bright as the day's light
A dragon has been unleashed
Get ready for the strife of your life
A fight is about to begin
Get your weapons ready
And your mind steady
Like acid rain the dragon's fire burns you till only your brain's left.

Ibby Armstrong (9)
Clapham Manor Primary School, Clapham

Laughter

Laughter is yellow like a pair of glittering fairy wings.
It sounds like twenty bells ringing a beautiful tune.
It smells like cherries freshly picked from the tree.
It feels like a smooth red apple ready to bite.
It tastes like a honey-flavoured cookie on my plate.
It reminds me of my pretty sister's Naming Day when laughter filled the air.

Lauren Barr (9)
Clapham Manor Primary School, Clapham

Laughter

Laughter is yellow like the beaming sun.
It sounds like a singer singing in mid-air.
It smells like a nice juicy apple just being bitten.
It feels like a smooth leaf tickling down my face.
It tastes like a sour orange being squeezed.
It reminds me of when I was tickled for the first time.

Michelle Salmon (9)
Clapham Manor Primary School, Clapham

D-Day

Bodies flying
Guns roaring
Gunships shelling
Men screaming
Bullets ricocheting
Paratroops diving
Snipers murdering
Hundreds dying
Death's traumatizing
Tanks missing
Soldiers wading
Mines slaughtering.
D-Day.

Finn Clarke (10)
Clapham Manor Primary School, Clapham

There Was A Teacher From Mooney

There was a teacher from Mooney
Who played like Wayne Rooney
He scored a goal
And fell in hole
They all called him Looney.

Jamille Malcolm (10)
Clapham Manor Primary School, Clapham

The Man From Dundee

There was an old man from Dundee,
Who fell out of a laughing oak tree,
He split his head
And passed away in bed
And that was the end of Brice Lee.

Onon Ihoeghinlan (11)
Clapham Manor Primary School, Clapham

Guess Who?

Royal saver
Brave adventurer
Ship lover
Barbossa hater
Stupid nutter
Silly shouter
Problem solver
Rum drinker
Apple eater
Cursed liver
Gold keeper.
Answer: Captain Jack Sparrow.

Sara Assad Mannings (10)
Clapham Manor Primary School, Clapham

A Bald-Headed Man From Dundee

There was a bald-headed man from Dundee,
His brother was called Bruce Lee,
He flew over to China,
Went to a diner,
Then ended up in Sydney.

Naoki Kishimoto-Eley (10)
Clapham Manor Primary School, Clapham

The Boy In Year Six

There was a boy in Year Six
Who made music better than Jimi Hendrix
He played the guitar
He was a star
But later choked on his sick.

Conrad Scott-Lee (11)
Clapham Manor Primary School, Clapham

Being Free

I wish I could fly like a bird
I wish I could soar through the sky
I wish I could fly as light as can be
I wish I could see all the world
I wish I could never cry
I wish I would never have a lover
I wish I would never have to hurry
I wish I could float around
I wish I could have fun all the time
I wish I could see all the dolphins
I wish I could leave this cage
I wish I would never worry
I wish I could walk the streets.

Samantha Culleton (10)
Clapham Manor Primary School, Clapham

The Playground

Line forming
Children singing
Trees waving
Football blazing
Basketball bouncing
Feet stamping
Tale telling
Adults talking
Toilets flushing
Girls slapping
Boys running
Children fighting
Teachers laughing
Puddle splashing
Bells ringing
Girls dancing
Whistle tooting.

Shannelle Vital (11)
Clapham Manor Primary School, Clapham

If I Saw A Fairy In The Playground

If I saw a fairy in the playground
I would be as happy as a clown
And we would fly to fairyland
And have fun together.

If I saw a fairy in the playground
I would make her my best friend
And she would always be there for me.

If I saw fairy in the playground
I would want her to grant me a wish
Of lots of friends just for me.

If I saw a fairy in the playground
She would be looking for me
Waiting for me outside
Ready to play with me.

Rudy Fordjuor (9)
Clapham Manor Primary School, Clapham

The Playground

Children playing
Footballs flying
Loudly screaming
Puddles splashing
Hands clapping
Boys running
Girls gossiping
Practising dancing
Climbing frame shaking
Toilets flooding
Trees balancing
Crazy stamping
Children crying
Whistle blowing
Time for lunch.

Zoe Deata Powell (11)
Clapham Manor Primary School, Clapham

Always Left Out

I'm all left out
Nobody cares
They think I'm a loser
They don't even share.

The teachers always pick the best
I feel so round
There's no one who picks me
Even when I'm down.

When they pick teams in the playground
Or whatever it is
I'm always lonely
And always like this.

If you pick teams, start with the worst
We won't be sad
Because we're not picked last
Now they're the ones with their faces down.

Ishara Bilson Graham (9)
Clapham Manor Primary School, Clapham

My Football

My football is precious.
My ball bounces and it's big.
It's special, secretive and silent.
It's a memory keeper.
This makes me happy when I'm down.
This is one of the best things I have.
It's a very bright, well behaved ball.
Has a brain filled with fame and glory.
Special to me, no one knows where it's been.
It makes the stars shine, it's the best.
It's a football winner.
It's the best ever.

Jason Nyarko (10)
Clapham Manor Primary School, Clapham

Aria

She has smooth, silky, soft fur.
A pink ribbon round her neck.
Her silver body shows how she's friendly.
She makes the perfect pet.

She will not scratch, she will not bite
With other animals
She does not fight,
Because she's as kind as a newborn baby.

Her small, smudged silhouette,
Glistens against the moonlight.
She walks around in total darkness.
She might give you a fright.

Calling to her friends,
Running in the garden,
Messages she has to send,
To her little companions.

She can jump as high as a tree.
(Please be careful)
She's as busy as a bee.
Rushing everywhere.

Eloise Magali Baker Lubac (9)
Clapham Manor Primary School, Clapham

My Mum

My mum is helpful, kind and caring.
She's the best in the world.
I make her laugh every day.
She's just so cool
She lets me stay up all night
I do a giant puzzle with her all the time.
She's smiley and happy all the time.
She's just so cool.

Amy Forbes (10)
Clapham Manor Primary School, Clapham

Running Round The Playground

Running round the playground
So much fun
Running round the playground
Eating a bun.

Running round the playground
Having a laugh
Running round the playground
I need a bath.

Running round the playground
Being very hyper
Running round the playground
Seeing a biker.

Running round the playground
Kicking a ball
Running round the playground
Hope I don't fall.

Running round the playground
I fell over
Running round the playground
I found a clover.

Felix Herreman-Deacon (10)
Clapham Manor Primary School, Clapham

A Bald-Headed Man From Dundee

A bald-headed man from Dundee,
Fell out of a crying oak tree.
He cracked his head
And passed away in his bed
That was the end of Tom Lee.

Patricia Thomas (10)
Clapham Manor Primary School, Clapham

Running On A Racetrack

Running on a racetrack,
Running on a racetrack,
Nothing, nothing, nothing,
Better than a racetrack.

Speeding past the rocks and rugs,
Speeding past the lazy bugs,
Nothing, nothing, nothing,
Faster than a racetrack.

Galloping through the racetrack,
Braying and neighing
Nothing, nothing, nothing,
Smoother than the racetrack.

Mean old stragglers swiftly
Running past,
Nothing, nothing, nothing,
Meaner than a racetrack.

Got to win the race, got to get the trophy,
Nothing, nothing, nothing,
Better than winning the racetrack.

Kirstie Wood (9)
Clapham Manor Primary School, Clapham

Two Brothers

There once were two brothers in school
One was clever, the other a fool,
When they went to work,
One was a jerk
And the other was Einstein's ghoul!

Hattie Bland (10)
Clapham Manor Primary School, Clapham

My Rainbow

My rainbow is like a parrot flying around like mad.
It's like a big bird flying freely in beauty.
When I shine my rainbow I am never sad.

Memories from Cornwall.
Important colours made from bubbles and liquids.
Red, green, blue and purple.

Special secrets, starry nights.
Some people think it's silly.
Then they start fights.

Blue ribbon, magnificent colours glow in the dark bubbles.
Great games to play.
Special to me.

Simple, shiny, seven colours on the side of the rainbow.
Not for you, just for me,
But I will share the beauty of the colours.

Charlotte Reddey (9)
Clapham Manor Primary School, Clapham

My Special Object

My special object is sometimes a troublemaker.
From the Greek word 'fresh blossom'.
Her outwardly confident nature hides a fragile and sensitive nature.
She's a breath of fresh air on a winter's morning.
Her adventures are endless like flying to Australia on a
one-winged plane.
She's a fighting machine as good as gold
I think she won the cup at four years old.
But she's my dog not yours,
She's the best and I wouldn't give her up at all.

Chloe Mathurin (10)
Clapham Manor Primary School, Clapham

Nobody Cares In The Playground

I'm so bored and lonely,
Nobody cares.
Nobody will let me play with them,
Nobody cares.
I walk down the hall,
Nobody cares.
Nobody's allowed in the popular hall where the cheerleaders are.
They even split the playground,
Nobody cares.
I'm sitting in the loos while I'm singing the blues.
Nobody cares.
Nobody cares.

Micah Sanatoro (9)
Clapham Manor Primary School, Clapham

There Was A Young Girl Called Isabel

There was a young girl called Isabel
Who owned a rather deep well
She fell to the bottom
And ripped her new cotton
And now she's decided to sell.

Zoe Dickey (11)
Clapham Manor Primary School, Clapham

Mad, Mad Mary

There once was a woman called Mary
Who thought she was a canary
She went to the shop
'Cause she had chickenpox
And was transported home by a fairy.

Keisha Fernandes (11)
Clapham Manor Primary School, Clapham

Fight In The Toilets

There's a fight in the toilets,
Boy versus boy,
It's a smacker
And face whopper,
It's a fight in the loo.

There's a fight in the toilets,
What am I to do?
Only me who knows,
No teachers know and certainly not you,
It's a fight in the loo.

There's a fight in the toilets,
A bruise here and there,
Who's going to win?
Who knows, not me, do you?
It's a fight in the loo.

There's a fight in the toilets,
A smack round the face,
A kick up the bum,
One on the floor, other in the toilet,
It's a fight in the loo.

There's a fight in the toilets,
Here comes the teacher,
Everyone out,
Run from the teacher,
Every boy for himself,
It's a fight in the loo.

There's a fight in the toilet,
In comes our teacher,
Detention all round,
Boy am I bored, I want out,
Finally the fight is over.

Ben Mesure (10)
Clapham Manor Primary School, Clapham

Hate

The taste of blood sucked up
Reminds you of the deep darkness as you walk through the midnight
Looks like a black hole
Feels like hurting somebody deeply
The colour of green snake slithering in the grass
Sounds like a lion roaring in the wilderness
Smells like the moon as cold as ice.

Jessica Nyarko (10)
Clapham Manor Primary School, Clapham

Sadness

A wailing shadow long forgotten,
Black like the pit down below.
Like tears shed by billions,
A desolate island, nothing left.
Rat corpses lying on the floor
A long-lost space unfilled.
Vast seas filled with darkness.

Jack Malone (9)
Clapham Manor Primary School, Clapham

Love

It smells like burning fire coming through you.
The colour looks like steaming red fire.
It sounds like a red sky blowing into your face.
It feels like a breaking heart that's just been broken into two pieces.
It tastes like blood burning through your teeth.
It looks like a dark deep hole with red all around it.

Kenisha Ferguson (9)
Clapham Manor Primary School, Clapham

The Playground

Running and jumping
Screaming and shouting
Twirling and hopping
Dropping and popping.

Children play
Teachers say, 'Hey!'
So they're sent to the wall
'It's always me,' says Paul.

The bell starts to ring
A-ling-a-ling-ling
Everyone in.

Then a child comes out
To play about
Teacher calling him in
So he starts running
Around and around till he falls down!

Kirsty Korley (10)
Clapham Manor Primary School, Clapham

Feeling Left Out

All alone, left alone.
Afraid and scared.
No joy, no happiness, no more for me.
Need a friend, need a group.
I feel left out.
No more friend or joy for me.
Getting bullied, people pushing.
I'm crying, no one knows or cares.
I feel left out.

Sara Moustahib (10)
Clapham Manor Primary School, Clapham

In The Playground

Children racing round the track
Others laughing, giggling, jumping
Girls gossiping, gossiping away
Boys patting the ball into the net.

All of a sudden a rabbit's in the way!
Children freeze around the track
Others stop laughing straight away.
Girls stop gossiping not even halfway,
While boys stop patting right away.

When all at once it hops into school
Then there's a herd running to chase it away,
This is terrible, it's in the caretaker's way
Then *swat, bang* . . . it hops out of view,
Phew!

Iheoma Anosike (10)
Clapham Manor Primary School, Clapham

Wayne Rooney

Everyone has his boots
He kicks the ball into
The goal and all the supporters cheer.

The crowd cheers when Rooney appears,
He scores the goal
That saves them all and now
They have won the Premiership Cup.

He plays for United
He's number eight.
So cheer for United
Because they're all great!

Nassim Boudjemaa (10)
Clapham Manor Primary School, Clapham

Snowy

My reindeer has brown bright eyes.
Her body is soft like snow.
Her ears green for the Earth's nature.
Her red rosy nose leading the way.
It's old so old I got it when I was a baby.

My mum bought it, we've loved it since.
It hangs on my wardrobe
It sits on my bed.
It's here with me as I'm writing this
Her inspiration is so creative and inventive.

Danielle-Marie Fowkes (10)
Clapham Manor Primary School, Clapham

Hate

A temperature like the burning sun.
A wet damp pit.
Red like the planet Mars.
The antlers of deer crashing together.
The tears like the salt in the sea.
A red-hot sweating face.
Crashing and banging on cars.

Nadira Ahmed (10)
Clapham Manor Primary School, Clapham

Fear

Fear, a chicken inside you, fast-beating heart.
A red hard heart with veins moving as fast as a cheetah.
Everything inside you is red like Mars
Reminds you of red blood.
Sound like lungs playing bumpy cars
Cold dipping water in a glass.
Looks like the sun sending flames down to Earth.

Matthew Addison/Mumuni (9)
Clapham Manor Primary School, Clapham

Darkness

Darkness all around
Black nothingness from space to the ground
Like being isolated in an empty space
Darkness, that's the case
It's black and lonely
In Hell there's darkness only
Now I see a beam of light
Now it is time to fight.

Jake Bertram-Kennedy (9)
Clapham Manor Primary School, Clapham

My Football Book

F ire plays in stadium
O ur Keane scores
O ur Scholes chips it over the goalie's head but
T he goalies say that is not good
B all bounces off the goalpost
A ttackers cry
L ocked in the dressing room at half-time
L ock the referee in.

Dylan Morris (10)
Clapham Manor Primary School, Clapham

Fear

A never-ending piercing scream ringing in your head.
A bitter lemon paralysing your soul.
A dark cave pouring with blood.
Black with bulbous yellow splodges flooding the floor.
Horrible stench rising up your nostrils.
Cold and sharp like needles.
Blurs of ghosts and dragons getting ready to
Pounce!

Liam Witchalls (10)
Clapham Manor Primary School, Clapham

In The Playground

In the playground trouble free,
Sitting alone just you and me.

If I were free, just you and me
We would sail across the seven seas.
We would jump and glide
With the greatest pride!

If I were free, just you and me
How happy we would be!
We would think about nothing but freedom.

Freedom's the word, it might sound absurd
But freedom's the word for you and
Me!

Zahra Chahboub (9)
Clapham Manor Primary School, Clapham

Playground

Playground fun
Playground run
Playground there's sun
Playground come.

Playground cheap
Playground steep
Playground hide
Playground seek.

Playground dance
Playground take a chance
Playground glance
Playground come from France!

Kieyar Hudson-Ford (10)
Clapham Manor Primary School, Clapham

A Poem About Anger

What colour is it?
It is orange like a fire.

What does it sound like?
It sounds like the building falling down from the fire.

What does it taste like?
It tastes like spicy chilli.

What does it smell like?
It smells like the smoke coming up from the air.

What does it look like?
It looks like a fire house.

What does it feel like?
It feels hot and the smoke feels soft.

What does it remind you of?
It reminds you of an exploding rocket.

Faijul Hakim (8)
Clapham Manor Primary School, Clapham

Anger

Anger is the colour red like Sherkan roaring for his prey on
All Souls Eve.

It sounds like zombies escaping from danger, running as slow
as clouds.

It smells like an iron burning a sheep's skin.
It feels like a hungry shark tearing my skin apart.
It tastes like burning bread, all crusty and black.
It reminds me of my brothers!

Hauwa Karaye (8)
Clapham Manor Primary School, Clapham

A Poem About Anger

It is purple like the plague.
It sounds like a meteor smashing on the ground.
It tastes like soggy pieces of paper.
It smells like hot flames of Hell.
It looks like a battle brewing.
It feels like a squidgy piece of soap.
It reminds me of a rotten, dead mouse.

Cian Jones (7)
Clapham Manor Primary School, Clapham

Anger

Anger is red like a dragon beaming fire.
Anger sounds like lava shooting out of a volcano.
Anger smells like steam coming out of an iron.
Anger feels like my head is going to explode.
Anger tastes like a burnt hot dog.
Anger reminds me of fire.

Sammy Ogunleye (8)
Clapham Manor Primary School, Clapham

Fun

Fun is blue like the sky on a clear day.
It sounds like children playing together.
It smells like a gust of fresh air that I breathe.
It feels like a bouncy ball that I can't catch.

Darren Bailey (8)
Clapham Manor Primary School, Clapham

Anger

Anger is red like a devil rising up from the Underworld.
It sounds like a wolf crying out for its mother.
It smells like control panels getting destroyed.
It feels like my veins rushing through my body.
It tastes like a watermelon, sweet and bitter.
It reminds me of me and my cousin screaming at each other.

Georgia Matthews (8)
Clapham Manor Primary School, Clapham

Anger

Anger is the colour red like a volcano erupting.
It sounds like a lion roaring.
It smells like dragon breath.
It feels like a spreading fire
It tastes like hot chilli pepper.
It reminds me of fighting with Harry.

Daniel Nagy (8)
Clapham Manor Primary School, Clapham

Laughter

Laughter is yellow like the gleaming sun.
It sounds like the sand swishing by the blue smooth sea.
It smells like the sand smoothly on the sea.
It feels like the sun bursting on me and tickling my skin.
It tastes yellow like a soft banana.
It reminds me of being in Jamaica when the sun is beaming on me.

Rukyrah Harris-Haughton (8)
Clapham Manor Primary School, Clapham

A Poem About Fear

What colour is it?
It's black like an exploding volcano.

What does it sound like?
It sounds like somebody opening a creaking door.

What does it taste like?
It tastes like cold water.

What does it smell like?
It smells like someone sweating.

What does it look like?
It looks like a disgusting chocolate rabbit.

What does it feel like?
It feels like a wave of cold.

What does it remind you of?
It reminds me of when I saw some people fighting in the park.

Mahinur Rahman Mohammed (8)
Clapham Manor Primary School, Clapham

A Poem About Love

It's orange like a murgh masala.
It sounds like my dad shouting, 'Here I am!'
It tastes like nice red fresh pimentos.
It smells like melted warm chocolate.
It looks like a chocolate rabbit.
It feels like a wave of warm water.
It reminds me of Russian dumplings.

Kuba Alchimowicz (8)
Clapham Manor Primary School, Clapham

A Poem About Love

What colour is it?
Pink like butterflies.

What does it sound like?
French music.

What does it taste like?
Romantic blush.

What does it smell like?
Floating bubbles.

What does it feel like?
Smooth cat fur.

What does it look like?
A bowl of fruit.

What does it remind you of?
Sweet chocolate.

Rebecca Norris (8)
Clapham Manor Primary School, Clapham

Music Kennings

Smooth stroker
Calm clasher
Bass boomer
Rough rapper
Sly saxer
Cool clarineter
Slim sister
Slippery singer
Dramatic drummer
Wild worder
Music.

Jeremy Taylor (10)
Clapham Manor Primary School, Clapham

Autumn Kennings

Leaves falling
Crimson floating
Others boating
Chills passing
Animals hibernating
Birds nesting
Scarves waving
Ponds freezing
People sneezing
Virus spreading
It's coming
Autumn good morning
Summer goodnight.

Amina Chahboub (11)
Clapham Manor Primary School, Clapham

A Poem About Fear

It is purple like glittery glitter.
It sounds like someone scattering glitter all over a piece of card.
It looks like a twinkling star shining in the sky.
It feels like my fingers and toes are all numb or frozen with ice.
It reminds me of icy frost and cross teachers!

Rahel Girma (8)
Clapham Manor Primary School, Clapham

The Teacher With Flat Fingers

A lovely teacher from Clapham,
Had twelve fingers and tapped 'em,
They all went flat
And looked like a mat,
A cat came over and sat on 'em.

Jasmin Niksic (11)
Clapham Manor Primary School, Clapham

Guess Who?

Personal protector
Family cooker
Clothes ironer
Music lover
Child liker
Room tidier
Money maker
Life saver
Homework helper
Brilliant dresser
Mum!

Samantha O'Keefe (10)
Clapham Manor Primary School, Clapham

The Colour Is Red

The colour is red like a fiery volcano.
It sounds like a charging bonfire.
It tastes like a hot chilli pepper.
It smells like smoky fire.
It looks like a three-headed monster.
It feels like blood.
It reminds me of me beating up my brother.

Olabode Balogun (7)
Clapham Manor Primary School, Clapham

A Poem About Love

It is pink like a rose that's growing from the ground.
It sounds like the beat of a heart.
It tastes like a soggy tomato taken from a wet glass.
It smells like roasting beef that my mum cooks.
It looks like a pink plum.
It feels like a soft bed.
It reminds me of my sweet mum.

Jade Bennett (8)
Clapham Manor Primary School, Clapham

Guess What?

Ticket giver,
Money taker,
Speed master,
Scream maker,
Sick clearer,
Loop turner,
Rail rider,
Cart mover,
Seat belt checker,
Helter skelter,
Queue maker.
Roller coaster.

Amy McIlveen (11)
Clapham Manor Primary School, Clapham

Limericks

There once was a girl called Sarina,
She wished she could be a ballerina,
She spun around,
Then fell to the ground,
How clumsy of Sarina.

Sarina Lee (10)
Clapham Manor Primary School, Clapham

Teacher

A member of staff called Miss Guest
She turned up to work in a vest
The children all giggled
She did a small wiggle
But she still gave the kids a SATs test!

Riki Koike (11)
Clapham Manor Primary School, Clapham

Fourteen Cats Kennings

Dog hater
Fabulous chaser
Furious killer
Milk lover
Quick eater
Long sleeper
Fast walker
Tree climber
Smelly popper
Idol runner
Mouse catcher
Fish eater.

Montana Paul (11)
Clapham Manor Primary School, Clapham

Anger

Anger is as red as a volcano breaking out.
It sounds like a white tiger roaring.
It smells like fire burning.
It feels like my head crashing against the wall.
It tastes peppery.
It reminds me of getting mad.

Kai Lewis (8)
Clapham Manor Primary School, Clapham

Laughter

Laughter is yellow like the shiny sun on a sunny day.
It smells like a flower opening its petals.
It feels like soft feathers in a pillow.
It tastes like a sweet apple on a tree.
It reminds me of happiness.

Eva Amato (8)
Clapham Manor Primary School, Clapham

Guess What . . . ?

Heavy rocker,
Peace stopper,
Soft composer,
Blues loser,
Guitar clouter,
Mad shouter,
Soulful singer,
Love bringer,
Jazz maker,
Vocal faker . . . it's music.

Callum Mackenzie (10)
Clapham Manor Primary School, Clapham

Silence

Silence is like the sea waving smoothly.
It sounds like a calm, empty room.
It smells like an ice cube melting very slowly.
It feels like the wind blowing through the freezing air.
It tastes like cold, icy water.
It reminds me of sleeping.

Hannah Bailey (8)
Clapham Manor Primary School, Clapham

Darkness

Darkness is black like an owl swooping down.
It sounds like lightning crashing.
It smells like smoke rising.
It feels like danger is near.
It tastes like black liquorice.
It reminds me of thunder.

Jessie Yates (8)
Clapham Manor Primary School, Clapham

Guess What? Kennings

Real squasher
Popcorn eater
Drink taker
Money maker
Ticket taker
PG stater
Trailer maker
Messy hater
TV wapper
Late timer
Cinema!

Cameo Coates (10)
Clapham Manor Primary School, Clapham

Darkness

Darkness is black like a werewolf howling at a full moon.
It sounds like a hollow chamber echoing darkness.
It smells like a cold sooty chimney.
It feels like an empty room when you're all alone.
It tastes like a rotten apple filled with worms slithering everywhere.
It reminds me of fear.

Leandre Burke (8)
Clapham Manor Primary School, Clapham

Fun!

Blue is a colour like the sky.
It sounds like a fan in my ears.
It smells like a dragon flying by.
It feels like the air blowing in my face.
It tastes like a nice pear.
It reminds me of the day he cried.

Raheem Whittaker (8)
Clapham Manor Primary School, Clapham

Anger

Anger is a strong red like a blazing furnace just being lit.
It sounds like a mother screaming after receiving displeasing news
about her child which is waiting to be born.
It smells like a candle which has just been extinguished.
It feels like a tattooing needle being pierced into your skin.
It tastes like eating a gallon of red pepper sauce.
Anger reminds me of grieving after a family member of a friend
has suddenly passed away.

Lauren Wright (9)
Clapham Manor Primary School, Clapham

Silence

Silence is light blue like the sky.
It sounds like the wind blowing slowly.
It smells nothing.
It feels wonderful and when you're lying down it feels smooth.
It does not taste of anything because you don't eat it.
Silence reminds me of people who live alone.

Jessica Costa (9)
Clapham Manor Primary School, Clapham

Anger

Anger is like blood in the sky.
It sounds like sucking people's blood when the moon comes out.
It smells like someone killing me.
It feels like my whole body is going to explode.
It tastes like sugar on a lollipop.
Anger reminds me of fighting.

Bussy Talabi (8)
Clapham Manor Primary School, Clapham

A Poem About Fear

Its colour is black like a ninja's fabric.
It sounds like somebody opening a creaky door.
It tastes like freezing water.
It smells like blood.
It looks like a running shower.
It feels like ice.
It reminds me of a sneaking ninja.

TJ Payne (7)
Clapham Manor Primary School, Clapham

Laughter

Laughter is blue like the sky on a hot day.
It sounds like ants giggling to each other.
It smells like people just finishing their Kentucky Fried Chicken.
It tastes like sweets flowing into my mouth.
It feels like a nice warm blanket.
Laughter reminds me of people laughing and enjoying themselves
on a beach.

Kai Chanter-Campbell (8)
Clapham Manor Primary School, Clapham

Anger

Anger is red like a bull in the Spanish Grand Prix.
It sounds like a volcano erupting in south Italy.
It smells like a dragon versus a brave knight.
It feels like travelling to planet Venus, the hottest place.
It tastes like 100° hot chocolate.
It reminds me of getting sunburnt in Spain.

Adham Mezmizi (9)
Clapham Manor Primary School, Clapham

A Poem About Anger

What colour is it?
It's red like blood on the floor.

What does it sound like?
It sounds like a burning volcano.

What does it smell like?
It smells like fiery fireballs.

It looks like a bullying butterfly.
It feels like crooked smoke.

What does it remind you of?
It reminds me of when I got
The blame for something I didn't do.

Harry Mesure (7)
Clapham Manor Primary School, Clapham

Danger

Danger is blue like the open sky.
It sounds like the snow blowing in the day.
It smells like flowers opening their petals.
It feels like the hot sun burning on the beach.
It tastes like hot chilli pepper.
Danger reminds me of someone jumping inside a volcano.

Nicalos Flowers (8)
Clapham Manor Primary School, Clapham

Hunger

Hunger is like a big fierce wave.
It sounds like a big brown bear roaring.
It smells like a dark cave.
It feels like my belly rumbling in darkness.
It tastes like an empty tummy calling for food.
Hunger reminds me of being empty for hours.

Leanne Davies (8)
Clapham Manor Primary School, Clapham

Fun

Fun is red and white and is very sporty,
It has lots of style and it is very dotty.

Fun is very exciting
But doesn't make me feel like fighting.

Fun tastes like ice cream
And makes me feel like I want to beam.

Fun sounds like a drum
But doesn't remind me of my rumbling tum.

Fun is like tapping a piano key
But I can have fun with you and me.

Fun reminds me of having exciting times
Not eating some rotten limes, yuck!

Vernon Anderson (9)
Clapham Manor Primary School, Clapham

Laughter

Laughter is yellow, like a romance in Paris.
It sounds like a comedian making everybody laugh in happiness.
It smells like a couple having a vanilla ice cream.
It feels like a wave of ripples in my tummy.
It tastes like a strawberry sundae floating in your mouth.
It reminds me of when I went to Ibiza.

Kadell Williams (8)
Clapham Manor Primary School, Clapham

Anger

Anger is red like the blood dripping from a vampire's mouth.
It sounds like a lion roaring in a battle.
It smells like a sewer monster's breath.
It tastes like slug juice slapping down your throat.
Anger reminds me of my brothers both bullying non-stop.

Navada Boston (8)
Clapham Manor Primary School, Clapham

Light Of The Fire

The light of the fire warms me
As I sit lonely and gloomily
Looking into space
With no one to talk to.

I sit there all alone
With not a soul to keep me company
I sit there and cry
As the sun in the sky beams into my window.

I think of the good times
When my friends were there for me
But now they're all gone.

I sit there until night
Gazing out of the window
Looking at stars
Feeling lonely inside.

Sofia Peixoto (10)
Henry Fawcett Primary School, Lambeth

Loneliness Of The Fly

I am the fly, going up to the stars like a bee buzzing.
Going to the bedroom, dark in the room.
Nervousness all around me.
Going to the lamp, happiness just zapped into me.
The lamp was on, I have the power from Heaven!
The light has made me so very happy.
The power has gone, the lamp has died!
Sadness, down in the dumps.
I go to the floor dying with sadness.

Alex Akamune (9)
Henry Fawcett Primary School, Lambeth

Nature And Animals

Nature is a beautiful sight.
I love nature.
My favourite animal is a cheetah.
My favourite insect is a beetle.
I love the open air of nature.
I love my garden because Mother Nature's world is free.

Helder Lopes (9)
Henry Fawcett Primary School, Lambeth

Journey Home From The Highlands

I looked out of the open window.
Cold breeze ran through my hair.
I heard the rushing of other cars.
The smell of petrol made my nose twitch.

The ravishing, radiant stars twinkled in the night sky,
Meadows and fields were lit up by them.

I was feeling impatient
Like a small child waiting to open up his Christmas presents.
Even more petrol hung in the air
As we pulled up at the petrol station.

I began daydreaming.
What would it be like to go to space?

The stars twinkled, the moon danced on high treetops.
It turned everything a ghostly blue.
It made me sleepy.
I could see my family.
I was sleepy, sleepy, sleepy,
Must sleep . . . sleep . . .

Danielle Millington (11)
Peter Hills with St Mary & St Paul's CE Primary School, Rotherhithe

My Car Journey Home

I peered out the window of the back seat,
A sunny sun shone bright and hot,
Glistening white and clear,
The clouds hung in the infinitely blue sky.

As I opened the window,
I heard rushing of cars and their roaring horns,
I saw people hurrying in and out of shops
And smelt leaking petrol flowing on the floor.

I daydreamed up into the sky,
My mind started to travel,
I asked,
'What would it be like to be a shopkeeper?'

Looking through the two front chairs,
The horn went *beep, beep, beep!*
I wondered would we ever get home,
To home, home, sweet home, home?

I started to get bored,
I started to get tired,
I started to get impatient and couldn't wait to get home.
My eyes started to get sleepy and so did I.

Then my eyes started to get really heavy,
Really heavy,
Really heavy,
Really . . .

Emily Saunders (10)
Peter Hills with St Mary & St Paul's CE Primary School, Rotherhithe

Coach Journey

I glanced up . . .
Sweet, green grass on the hilltop was blowing in the breeze.
Charming cows and calves
With the fit farmer travelling through the trees.
Ride, coach, ride.
Ride, coach, ride.
Magnificent Mercedes and vicious vans rushed on the motorway.
Children skipped sensibly doing as they may.
Ride, coach, ride.
Ride, coach, ride.
I turned round.
Are we held hostage?
Well, I am really not sure.
Roller coaster rides, great games, fantastic food.
I wonder if there was more.
Ride, coach, ride.
Ride, coach, ride.
I gazed down.
The glittery sunrays burnt my arm.
As we entered the modern city I started to be calm.
Ride, coach, ride, Hastings here we come.
Ride, coach, ride, Hastings here we come.
I took off my seatbelt.
I snatched my handbag off the coach and I went.
I wondered what hotel we were going to rent.
Bye, coach, bye, we have arrived at Hastings.
Bye, coach, bye, we have arrived at Hastings.

Jeneba Brewah (11)
Peter Hills with St Mary & St Paul's CE Primary School, Rotherhithe

Coach To Cardiff

I looked out of the window,
And could see acres of fields
Covered with a blanket of yellow flowers.
Sounds of other cars rushed past,
I could smell mixed aromas of food flying in the air.
The racket of the frantic footballs fans
Shouting and chanting on the coach.
How long until we arrive? I thought to myself
Making pictures of cars and people
In the wonderful white cotton clouds
Turning with the world as it spins.

The journey carried on and my belly turned.
My eyes were heavy and I thought to myself,
We are almost there now
We are almost there now
We are almost . . .

Teddy Lands (10)
Peter Hills with St Mary & St Paul's CE Primary School, Rotherhithe

Aeroplane To Spain

I looked out the wide windows,
White, fluffy clouds frolicked by.
The smell of freshly cooked muffins flooded the huge aeroplane.

Faint sounds of the cabin crew calling out.
I stared at the fluffy clouds trying to make pretty pictures.

When will this boring journey be over?

Cassie Prescott (10)
Peter Hills with St Mary & St Paul's CE Primary School, Rotherhithe

A Journey To Hythe

I gazed out the window
And saw the sun glistening
On the stunning beach in Hythe.

All I could smell was putrid petrol
Pumping from the back of the engine.

Cars were zooming past
Faster than a rocket
Heat ran through my veins like blood
I was bored and tired
Then I fell asleep.

The expedition ended
I felt the coldness of my mum
The tips of her hand rolled round me
Like a blowing breeze.

I was there at my nan and grandad's house
I was happy, happier than I had ever been.

Star Cronin (11)
Peter Hills with St Mary & St Paul's CE Primary School, Rotherhithe

An American Cruise

I peered out of the window,
Endless blue sea stretched around me.
I felt the gentle touch of the breeze blowing from afar.

Smells of pukey petrol poured off the boat,
Blue, salty water surrounded me,
I saw rolls of wavy warm water slide after the boat.

I was jolly as I was being lowered down in shark-infested water.
Sharks waited for me eagerly,
As they glided swiftly through the water.

William Mode (11)
Peter Hills with St Mary & St Paul's CE Primary School, Rotherhithe

Round The Rink

Sliding on ice
All cold and bare
I was impatient, irritated
Waiting there.

Figure skaters danced
Showing off their skill
I tried to follow them, copy them
A thought, a thrill.

It's a freezing Friday
But I don't care
Ice skating perfection
Is what I don't dare.

I daydream
To be on ice
A chance, a thought
A dream come true would be nice.

Gliding and spinning
Every day and night
I'd be a movie star on ice
Me in the spotlight.

Going round the rink
Strutting my stuff
Roses being thrown
That would be enough.

Round the rink
Round the
Round
Rink.

Courtnie Ashman (10)
Peter Hills with St Mary & St Paul's CE Primary School, Rotherhithe

Walking With The Dead Through A Graveyard

I step through a stubbly, stony path,
Crunch! Crunch!
Shivers running down my spine,
Bats gliding above my head.

Human blood,
Human flesh,
Human bones,
And as quick as a cheetah
Out popped the dead.

Sharp axes and knives,
Powerful guns and swords,
Crunched-up graves all over the floor.

It was very scary,
Their faces were all red
And their arms were all hairy.

I looked back and forward,
Left and right,
Luckily there wasn't a spooky zombie in sight.

Until . . .

Joe Sullivan (11)
Peter Hills with St Mary & St Paul's CE Primary School, Rotherhithe

A Car Journey To Cardiff To See My Favourite Football Team

Looking out of my uncle's van
I ate and drank and stared at the sunny sky
The smell of petrol was seeping up my nose
As the houses passed
I was getting more and more anxious to get there

When in the car the wheels were scraping the ground
Like chalk on a whiteboard
I was thinking, *will we get there? Who will win?*
A shivery feeling shot up my spine
The car might crash

I came out of my trance
The car stopped
We were there
This was the moment
The stadium stood up, vast, sparkling in my eyes.

Joe Turner (11)
Peter Hills with St Mary & St Paul's CE Primary School, Rotherhithe

On The Way To Arsenal

Sitting in the terrible traffic
Looking out the wet window
People pushing past
Drivers getting angry
Places to be
Walking down the street
Cheers can be heard
Arsenal, Arsenal, Arsenal
Makes me smile
The football ground in the distance
Passing by shops with people shopping
Pubs on corners, people drinking
Not far now, nearly there!

Jake Martin (11)
Peter Hills with St Mary & St Paul's CE Primary School, Rotherhithe

The Journey On A Cruise

I peered out my bedroom window,
The dolphin's skin was glistening as it followed the boat,
Wet, white waves collided with themselves
Against the cruise ship.
I could smell the salty sea drifting in the distance.
Delicious food hit my face.
I was tempted.

The calm blue sea settled on the shore.
In my mind I was relaxing on the golden beaches
In the Caribbean.
Faces of the young and elderly,
I wondered what they were like?

The boat was being carried as gently as a baby from its grand cot.
I was restful,
I was restful,
I was,
I . . .

Cydney Colton (11)
Peter Hills with St Mary & St Paul's CE Primary School, Rotherhithe

My Journey Through Greenwich Tunnel

I strolled into the tunnel like a proud queen,
The lift arrived,
As I sat down my belly turned over,
The metal lift entered to the ground floor,
Everyone rushed out of the lift,
Pushing to get out of the terrifying tunnel.

Round, metal walls with cracked pipes,
Water from pipes dripping on the dirty, white-tiled floor,
As water splashed on the outside of the walls,
I wondered what it would be like
To live under the wild, waving water
As I walked faster my legs started to ache
And I started to get a high temperature,
Only a tiny breeze came in from the air conditioning.

I started to daydream about fish surrounding us under the water,
Sweating as I ran along to catch up with my aunty,
Suddenly we are out of the tunnel and into familiar fresh air.

Jade Negus (10)
Peter Hills with St Mary & St Paul's CE Primary School, Rotherhithe

Through Chistlehurst Caves

Drip, drip, crunch, crunch!
It was all I could hear.
The drip from the rusty tap,
The squeak of the putrid, running rat,
The crunch of my dirty shoes,
My feet felt like super glue.

In my confusion I bumped into the gungy well,
I think it went right down to Hell.
My lantern turned off,
Someone started to cough,
But when I turned around no one was there!

I felt so alert but I fell in the dirt,
I looked up and saw a face carved in the wall.
A shiver ran right down my spine.
Its eyes bored straight into mine.
'Ami!' my mum called.
I started to run out of the tunnel
And into the sun.

Ami Alexandria Andrews-Rafe (10)
Peter Hills with St Mary & St Paul's CE Primary School, Rotherhithe

Bumpy Ride

I turned round.
Everyone on the coach was sleeping and snoring.
Bright stars winked as we drove past.
The silver moonlight brushed my face
As I realised the moon was following us.
As it got later I got hungrier.
My belly began to rumble.
My legs ached as my sister lay on them.
But I felt too tired to move.
Old Spanish music filled the air
And drifted through my ears.
My mind started to travel.
Would we ever get to the hotel?
Bored, I fiddled with my bag.
I found my radio and turned it on.
I had completely forgotten I was in Spain.
Expecting to hear my favourite songs
I was in for a surprise.
More Spanish music filled the air.
With anger I threw the radio away.
The coach got warmer
And my eyes started to shut.

Jacqueline Ilumoka (11)
Peter Hills with St Mary & St Paul's CE Primary School, Rotherhithe

The Roller Coaster

I looked down
People were ants angrily
Scuttling on the ground

A fresh taste of wind
Whistled into my mouth

My eyes closed shut
I was falling off
A colossal cliff

Twists and turns made
Me feel sick
My heart beat like the
Thump of an elephant's
Foot smashing the
Ground.

The ride got slower, slower
Then stopped.

Freddie Newbery (10)
Peter Hills with St Mary & St Paul's CE Primary School, Rotherhithe

Friends

Friends can be bossy
And some you can't trust,
Some are show-offs and quite rude.
If you want to have a friend you've got to check
That the person suits your tastes.

Some can be jealous of what you've got,
Some can act like they're older than you
But they're not.

You've got to keep clear of friend snatchers,
And be best friends quick,
You've got to be brave about everything.

If you're bullied because you have a friend,
Stand up for your rights and stand up for yourself.
These are tips about friends.

Mary Anifowose (9)
St John's CE Primary School, Walworth

My Best Friend

Kadeen is the best friend ever,
We'll never break up, never,
She always gives me presents,
And we both like pheasants.

Kadeen is the best friend ever,
She's really funny and really clever,
If I fall down,
She won't frown.

Kadeen is the best friend ever,
We always play together,
We always play run and catch,
And she's never a crosspatch.

Kadeen is the best friend ever,
She's as pretty as a peacock's feather,
She's also kind and sweet,
We chatter whenever we meet.

Katy Linkens (9)
St John's CE Primary School, Walworth

Tooth Fairy Wanted

Must be brave,
Must have deep blue
Wands to wave.
Must be quick and
Must be clever.
Must not wake
A human *ever!*

Must like danger,
Must be strong,
(Human teeth are large and long)
Must be good at
Finding things.
Must have dark
And silent wings.

Must not fear
The dog or cat.
Must not mind
A top floor flat.
Must know how
To read and write
Notes - *without*
A glow-worm's light.
Must not play
With children's toys,
(Cars and bears
Can make a noise.)
Must enjoy
Exciting flights.
Nasty scares and
Awful frights.

If you have the
Skills we need,
(Courage, quietness
And speed)
Join our midnight
Team today . . .
Ring our bell
And flap this way.

We will give our
New collectors
Bags of coins
And tooth detectors.

Sabrina Brown (9)
St John's CE Primary School, Walworth

Katy

Katy's fabulous,
Katy's cool.
Katy's excellent,
We all know Katy rules.
Katy's smart,
Katy's nice,
Yep! Katy is the one that never hates mice.
Katy's never bad,
Katy's never sad,
Katy's never made anyone ever so sad.
She's my best friend in the whole school,
I hope nobody takes her away,
We could live together with our own pool,
So I really like Katy I say.
She's a better friend than Laura,
And Chantel,
Plus Katy can spell.
So now you know all about Katy,
She's the queen of best friends as you can see.

Katy is the best,
Better than the rest.
I like her so much,
As you can see.
Katy, Katy, if you're reading,
If I do something bad please forgive me,
As much as I forgive you.
I don't care if we might go to different secondary schools,
Or if we turn into fools,
We'll be best friends forever and ever.

Kadeen Thomas (9)
St John's CE Primary School, Walworth

Brave Soldier

What can you see?

Bombs brightening the dark night sky, people will eventually die.
Bodies rotting on the ground,
Will they ever be found?
Aeroplanes flying quickly in the sky,
When you see them you think you're going to die.
Bullets from all sides,
Soldiers trying to find a place to hide.

What can you feel?

Feeling scared I might die,
I will hope my spirit goes up into the sky.
Feeling hungry, haven't eaten in hours,
So hungry I could eat flowers.
Feeling lonely and really sad,
Feel like I am going mad.

What can you hear?

I can hear soldiers screaming in pain,
It is as loud as a train.
Tanks moving very near,
That's when you feel the fear.
Bombs exploding on every side,
You can just hear the sea's tide.

Harvey Green (11)
St John's CE Primary School, Walworth

Seaside Poem

What can you see?

I see tourists walking by,
In the morning I see the clear blue sky.
Sometimes fish glide through the ocean,
All of them swim in slow motion.
Everywhere there's golden sand,
A few metres away from me there's a candyfloss stand.

What can you feel?

I feel scared because people can catch me in a net,
Then there will be no water for me to stay wet.
I feel happy because I live near the sea,
I love my life because I can swim free.
I feel hungry, I can only eat kelp,
But it's not easy to find, I need help.

What can you hear?

I hear children splashing in the sea,
I hear adults having a cup of tea.
I hear seagulls screaming above me,
I also hear the quiet, calm sea.

Harrison Gray (11)
St John's CE Primary School, Walworth

I Am The Bright Sun

What can I see?

Glittering blue sea,
It's fun for you and me,
Sloppy, wet sand,
Children building sandcastles.
The sea is very calm,
Lifeguards watching everyone,
People frying themselves under me,
Children running up and down.

What can I feel?

I am very happy because I am the light for everyone,
I am very bright and warm,
I'm feeling hot, hot, hot.
I don't want anyone to touch me,
I'm hot, hot, hot.

What can I hear?

People chewing on their sandwiches,
The waves swishing from side to side,
Voices of children,
People having fun.
Dolphins swimming, having fun,
While fishes go down to have fun as well.

Staresha Smith (10)
St John's CE Primary School, Walworth

Brave Soldier

I see enemy troops not far but near,
I say, 'Prepare, men, just do not fear.'
A sea of bullets flies through the sky,
I start to tremble, I start to cry.
I see blazing fire rise through the sky,
Why do people fight? Oh, I wonder why.
Red poppies fill the field,
The beautiful field of Flanders Field.
Bullets fly overhead,
People shot, they fall down dead.

I hear guns banging, bang and bang,
When will this ever end?
But I shall fight for our lives and our beautiful wives.
Blazing fires fill the skies,
I hear people burning and eventually dying.
Flares flying up ahead,
People dying, they fall down dead.
I know what will happen,
I now begin to tremble, not only me but all.
I tremble because we may not win this war.
People killing, people dying,
Children hurt, I hear them crying.

I'm shocked why people can't be,
Be nice to me and our country.
I cry and cry but people still die and die,
But I shall stand brave.
I will win this war on my grandad's grave.

Samuel Ametewee (11)
St John's CE Primary School, Walworth

The Blitz Brits

The terrifying Blitz has come around,
Destroying our poor town,
I see bombs exploding, flashing before my eyes,
Fire spreading quicker and quicker while all the flames flicker,
Planes over on top of my head,
Flying and flying over my bed.
Air raid sirens going off,
And the wardens shouting,
'Get into your Anderson shelters.'
I see gunshots being fired,
As I watch and stare.

I am crying and crying all through the night,
No one to kiss me or say goodnight,
Sadder and sadder by the minute as I drift off to sleep,
But I can still feel the sadness.
I am upset my mum is not here, while my dad's at war,
And no one to cuddle and say, 'It will be alright.'
I scare myself all day long, how could this happen?
But I knew all along,
My time would come.

I hear guns getting lighter and lighter,
I can hear the birds chirping as the sun goes down.
The air raids are starting to stop but it is still ringing in my ears.
The wardens go back to their posts,
Children come out to play and pray while others weep.
These are my last words I must say,
'I love my mum and my dad
But now I must say goodnight as I drift off with the angels.'

Emma Barnard (11)
St John's CE Primary School, Walworth

Summer

What can you see?

Singing sun, beautiful flowers,
Puffy white clouds moving like cowards.
Blazing grass, long green trees,
In the sky are flying bees.
Seagulls flapping, birds singing,
Clouds shaped like bells ringing.
Beautiful flowers in the ground,
Flying bees all around.

What can you feel?

Cool breeze in the air,
The sun is sizzling everywhere.
Happy clouds make you see,
How happy they can be.
The sun is happy with a blaze,
On the grass a shining phrase.
The sun is warm, the sun is hot,
Boiling like a saucepan pot.

What can you hear?

Seagulls squawking, dogs barking,
Bees are there making their marking.
Birds singing, wind blowing,
Farmers are there, seeds sowing.
Flowers swishing, people talking,
People stamping and walking.
Flowers shooting, seagulls squawking,
People tapping and stacking.

Simone Nyame (10)
St John's CE Primary School, Walworth

What Is A Million?

The tiny ants
You find in an oak tree.
The many fish that
Swim in the ocean.

One hundred centipedes
Crawling in a line.
Brightly coloured
Tulips that came from Amsterdam.

A hundred times five thousand spiders
That live underground.
The school children in west Africa
All in uniform.

Tiny cells in our bodies
Making us see, hear, smell, touch and taste.
Germs in the air
Dancing all around us trying to take over.

Shanny Joy Nicol-Dundas (8)
St John's CE Primary School, Walworth

I Am The Ocean

Exotic fish with shiny scales,
Sea horses, dolphins and whales fighting for their lives,
Sharks lurking for their prey,
Mermaids combing their golden locks away,
Glittering shells lying at the bottom of the sea,
Divers searching for what they can see,
Old shipwrecks with treasure to hide,
From Treasure Island where the pirates could not find.

I am calm as I am the ocean,
But sometimes I can cause commotion,
I rock the boats with my terrible anger,
Waves rise up and the boats go under.

Children laughing on the sand,
Which is a place I do not know as it is called no-man's-land,
Seagulls squawking their brains away,
Trying to take my fish away.

Ruthanne Fasanya (10)
St John's CE Primary School, Walworth

In The War

Bombs exploding like balls of fire,
Bullets flying in the sky.
Whimpering people lying on the ground,
Deep red puddles all around.
School wasn't better, that's for sure,
I'm already in trouble as I walk through the door.
Quite a few canings, I'm used to it,
Everyone wide-eyed, dribbling spit.

I feel so scared on the way home,
Just in case something has happened.
When I arrive my luck refills,
As Mother is in the shelter knitting.
I give her a kiss, two or three,
And all of a sudden she says she loves me.

Distant cries,
I'm not surprised,
I can hear bombs dropping quite near.
Mother and I run into the shelter,
She soothes me with her singing
And says, 'We're going to make it.'
I almost believe her,
But at this time no one can be sure.

Leah Buckle (10)
St John's CE Primary School, Walworth

At The Sea

Children playing in the sand,
Like it's their little land,
Crabs running to the sea,
To hide from me,
Bright colours in the sea,
For me to see,
Seagulls diving for their prey,
Before May.

Sometimes I'm happy,
Sometimes I'm sad,
Sometimes I don't know what I am,
The soft sand on my feet,
Has a lot of heat,
The calm sea,
Soothes my soul with glee,
The wavy sea sets me free.

Children laughing with joy,
Some with toys,
Splashing in the water,
Flies to the sand,
Dolphins squeaking,
To win the race,
Oh, what a wonderful day!

Chela Auguste (10)
St John's CE Primary School, Walworth

My Summer Holidays

I am lying on the beach,
Turning bright as a peach.
I see the yellow beach full of shells,
People sniffing the lovely smells.
The blue sparkling sea,
That is splashing on me.
The sun is shining in my eyes,
People lying on their thighs.
Little crabs walking across,
Looking like they are lost.

I am feeling happy, having fun,
Lying down in the hot sun.
Relaxing while I am sunbathing,
And a chocolate ice cream I am craving.
I am under the bright sun feeling warm,
Not cold and shivery like a storm.
I feel really tired,
After the sights I have admired.
I want to go around again,
Before my summer holiday ends.

I can hear children playing,
While I am calmly laying.
I hear children bashing buckets together,
I hear parents saying, 'Is that racket going to last forever?'
I hear aeroplanes in the sky,
As they take off and start to fly.
I hear the waves slapping against the rocks,
And the boats rowing to the docks.
I hear peaceful sounds,
Not like flicking bands.

Helen Gaughan (10)
St John's CE Primary School, Walworth

Big Red Bus

Driving through the busy roads,
Stopping at the bus stops.
Seeing all the signs around,
And all the different houses about.
I see black roads up ahead,
I also can see people's heads.
Now I know that's where a bus stop lies,
So I better get ready to *stop!*

The bell vibrating in my ears like a fire alarm,
People walking up and down.
Heavy footsteps getting on, this is what I can feel,
People hopping on for a ride.
I feel happy because I can take them to where their destiny lies.

The bus driver opening and shutting the doors,
People paying their bus fare.
The bell going *ring-a-ding-ding* telling me to stop,
People talking and joking about. This is what I can hear.
People pressing their horns outside,
The engine going as we stop.

I love this job very much,
And I would never give it up.

Hayley Woods (11)
St John's CE Primary School, Walworth

Why Throw Litter On Me?

I'm the street who likes to be neat,
But all I see is people eat,
And all they do is drop their food,
But sometimes I'm not in the mood,
All I can see is litter on me,
I wish this would never be.

I feel angry all the time,
Oh! Some people just cross the line,
If some people hear me scream,
They will think it's just a dream,
I feel sad because people drop things on me,
I hate my life, it just can't be.

I hear wrappers scrunch like crackers,
Hear it screech, hear it scratch,
I hear sticks, I hear stones,
They break my bones.

Elizabeth Olufowora (11)
St John's CE Primary School, Walworth

Playground Menace

See

I see boys playing loudly,
I see girls skipping quickly.
Boys and girls getting told off.
What can I see?
A big, fat bumblebee.

Feel

I feel bad for my mother,
I feel sad for my father,
I feel selfish because I got a friend in trouble.

Hear

I hear 500 children shouting loudly,
I don't know what to do.
Girls crying horribly in the playground,
Boys making a lot of sound.
Bells ringing a lot of times,
And all of those footballs are mine.
I hear footballs bouncing on the ground,
I always score from a rebound.

Luke Robinson (10)
St John's CE Primary School, Walworth

Athena's Poem

What can you see?

Gods and goddesses drinking wine,
Watching people on Earth growing vine.
Olympia and Sparta are having a vicious war,
Whilst Aires is helping Sparta and Zeus is firing bolts.

What can you feel?

I'm worried about Olympia and Sparta -
What will happen when this chaos is over?
I feel very fed up at always having wars,
Why can't people do other things like killing lots more boars?

What can you hear?

I can hear people screaming whilst Aires is beaming.
Zeus is shouting tremendously
And people are crying over loved ones' dead bodies.

Leah McKay (11)
St John's CE Primary School, Walworth

British War

I can see people falling and crying loudly.
I can see people shooting roundly.
I can see bright bombs exploding.
Soldiers running rapidly, not to be found.
Blood spilling on the ground.

I feel hurt because people die.
I feel people running past me for their lives.
I feel sad, I really want to cry.
How do I feel? I feel like a captain.

I hear people screaming ferociously.
I hear captains shouting horridly.
I hear guns banging randomly.
I hear soldiers' footsteps stamping.
What I mostly hear is the cry of joy when the war ends.

Jo-Caleb Damoah (10)
St John's CE Primary School, Walworth

The Diver

I put on my aqua tank and suit,
Exploring like a ship with a wooden keel,
The secrets of the sea. Along my lazy road
On and on I swim -
Over wavy seas that with a touch explode,
Into shrimps, then closing rock to the music of the tide,
Over tiny sea creatures that disappear in puffs of sand.
Look, a group of pearls bubbling at my side,
Breaks on my palm -
Those pearls are my everything! . . . Does that hole hide
Some old Amadian shipwreck in seaweed furled,
Crusted with rocks, her cannon old and rusty?
The great Senora Phillipa? What treasures in her hold?
Jewels and a million bars of solid gold?
Shall I ever know? Too soon comes the closing cold,
Catches on my flesh and limb,
And drags me to the sandy surface. Freezing, back I swim,
To the seaside, the noisy bathers, the ordinary world.

Jessica Mensah (10)
St John's CE Primary School, Walworth

Friends

Friends can be funny and make you laugh,
When they are silly I say, 'Don't be daft.'
I admire them very much in every way,
I like the way they giggle and sing,
At Christmas, on birthdays great cards they bring.
We go to school, we learn and play,
When I'm in school I'll have a great day.

Some people don't have any,
But they would like to have many.
They sit down at lunchtimes all alone,
Kicking and throwing different stones.
Oh, how they would wish, looking into the sky,
Can't everyone have friends? Tell me why.

Sophie Whitlock (10)
St Joseph's School, Rotherhithe

You Will Always Be In My Dreams!

When I found out,
That you only had nine months to live,
Watching you die in pain,
Seeing all the years of fun,
Flowing down the drain.
It was hard at first,
But I wouldn't let anyone know it,
Although it was harder not to show it.
When you passed away,
With everyone crowded round the bed,
With nothing said,
Just a teardrop instead.
The funeral came,
When you were in slumber,
As Robbie finished another number.
You will always be in my dreams,
Till we meet again, Tracey.

Katie Smyth (11)
St Joseph's School, Rotherhithe

Why?

Why has this happened?
All those lives have been taken away
Families are grieving
Kids separated from parents.

Why has this happened?
Houses are destroyed
People are fearful
Another tsunami might happen.

Why has this happened?
People endeavouring to find their families
Bodies not found yet
People worrying if their families and friends are alive.

Why has this happened?
People feeling heartbroken
Wondering if they're cursed
Their lives will never be the same again
Why has this happened?

Shukura Brown (10)
St Joseph's School, Rotherhithe

Why Did You Abandon Me?

Being thrown from one person to another,
Different fathers, different mothers.
No one cares for me like my mum does,
They don't know about true love.

Why did my mum abandon me?
Couldn't she handle me?
For some reason, deep down in my heart,
There's something telling me to keep loving her,
Even though we are far apart.

Moving houses, moving places,
New friends, new faces.
Here we go again, packing up our bags,
All I want is my mum back!

I had no relationship with my dad,
But it wasn't so upsetting.
He left me when I was small,
I didn't have a clue.

I am with a new family,
They're called the Hennesys.
They are great fun,
But not as much pleasure as my mum.

Doreen Boateng-Amponsah (10)
St Joseph's School, Rotherhithe

Dad, That Three Letter Word

That three letter word, *dad*
Will always exist in my world.
But in the real world confusion is upon me
And dad does not exist.

We had good times
We had bad times.
But my mum and I loved him
And he loved us back.

He made me a man
But now he is gone.
I wish my dad could come back
To see how I am.

Dad was like a big brother
With all the fun and charm.
But now he is gone
It is just not the same.

Dad, that three letter word
I will never forget.
You will always exist in my world
But in the real world confusion is upon me
Because you are not here.

James Osei (10)
St Joseph's School, Rotherhithe

Why Did You Go, Dad?

I pleaded with you not to go,
Where are you?
You don't even ring anymore,
Dad, why did you go?

I wonder where you are while I'm writing this,
I can't even remember the last time you came round.
I brood about you night and day,
Dad, why did you go?

I can remember the day you left,
When you took your last breath in front of me.
When you suggested you were leaving I couldn't bear it,
Dad, why did you go?

Was it because of me?
Honestly, I would do anything to get you back.
You were the best dad anybody could ask for,
Dad, why did you go?

Whenever I hear the door knock I think it's you,
I dash to the door but it's somebody else.
Nobody talks about you anymore,
Dad, why did you go?

Ami Metcalf (10)
St Joseph's School, Rotherhithe

My White, Empty Room

I live in a white, empty room
In my head.
I was in an accident,
Knocked down by a car.
Mum's always crying,
Dad doesn't visit.
If only I could speak my mind.

Sometimes I get a feeling that it's the day
When I wake up.
But my eyes start to close frantically
Into a deep, deep sleep.
If only I could speak my mind.

The day has come
That I will wake up.
I can feel my bones arising.
I can feel the cold winter's breeze
Touching my hair.
My eyelashes start to shiver.
My eyelids awaken.
My smile starts.
I try to find my voice.
A word feels like it's breaking out.
'Mum, I love you.'

Hannah Sofoluke (10)
St Joseph's School, Rotherhithe

I Don't Care

I don't care
After all, you're a stranger to me,
You left me
Before I was even born.
Can't you just visit me
At least once?
In the morning, maybe,
Or a birthday even.

You don't know me,
You don't know
How it feels not having a dad.
Him not even knowing
His own daughter.
I don't even know who you are.
I know it in my heart,
That there's an empty part,
Gloomy with sadness,
But only one person
Can fill it up with happiness.

Natalie Marshall (11)
St Joseph's School, Rotherhithe

A Day In London Town

I wake up one morning,
In sight of London's Strand.
I wonder who is going to be
The first to lift their nose in pride?

I slowly get up from the gutter
I have been in.
I pick up my belongings, the little I have,
I start to hobble
With bags in hand.

It is lunchtime
Big Ben strikes twelve.
Everyone rushes to Starbucks.
The streets are lonely.
I check in the bins for bread.
My eyes are terribly glued.

I see a posh man walk past
With a Marks & Sparks food bag.
I have no food.
Why can't they just spare a piece of bread
For a ravenous young man?

Joe Hatch (10)
St Joseph's School, Rotherhithe

My Dad's Bad Back

My father's got a bad back
He loves me
He does not lie on a sick bed
Or stay in hospital.

My father slaves and slaves at work just for me
To give me a good life,
I love my dad.

My dad gives me love and consideration
He works so hard and doesn't slack
He cherishes me
But I know he can avoid the pain.

He's got three children and me
A good family to support him
I think my dad's the best dad in the world.
I love my dad.

Nii Bruce-Tagoe (11)
St Joseph's School, Rotherhithe

I Like Drawing

I like drawing funny faces that make me laugh.
I like drawing, it's never boring.
I think drawing is the best.
I like drawing first thing in the morning,
Late in the evening till I go to bed.
I like drawing cartoon faces
In different sizes and different places.
It makes me feel cool.
I like drawing best of all.

Biola Adeyemo (10)
St Joseph's School, Rotherhithe

Dad, Dad

Dad, Dad, why did you leave?
Because you are so precious to me.
I don't know why you left.
I want you back, Dad.
But you won't tell me why.
If you tell me I can make things better
For you and Mum.
All I want is you and Mum
To be with each other
So we can have a happy family.
We are not coping without you
Because you are so special to all of us.
Dad, please come back to us.
We all love you so much,
You don't know how much we love you.
We can do fun things together,
But when you are not there we cannot have fun.
We all want you back, Dad, not to have fun,
But because we love you.
Dad, you broke my heart when you left.

From Bobby.

Bobby Pettengell (11)
St Joseph's School, Rotherhithe

I Am Afraid . . .

I am afraid of running wild boars creeping through the woods.
I am afraid of stinging bees buzzing in the sky.
I am afraid of thumping gorillas hitting logs.
I am afraid of the terrifying Loch Ness monster
Swimming in the sea.
I am afraid of terrifying heights
Because they are way up in the sky.
I am afraid of cheetahs zooming in the wild.

Liam Wood (7)
Stewart Fleming Primary School, Anerley

It Was So Quiet

It was so quiet that I heard the sun beaming in the air.
It was so quiet that I heard air floating through the sky.
It was so quiet that I heard a mole digging through the ground.
It was so quiet that I heard my heart inside my body.
It was so quiet that I heard the floorboards squeaking.
It was so quiet that I heard the grass blow in the gentle breeze.
It was so quiet that I heard leaves falling from the autumn trees.

Lucy Osmond (7)
Stewart Fleming Primary School, Anerley

Christmas Senses

Christmas looks like snowflakes falling from the sky.
Christmas sounds like sleigh bells jingling in the sky.
Christmas tastes like crumbly mince pies.
Christmas smells like roast turkey cooking in the oven.
Christmas feels very happy.

Katherine Roth (8)
Stewart Fleming Primary School, Anerley

Football Crazy

F ootball crazy
O n the football pitch
O ver the keeper
T he ball's gone in
B ooing from the away crowd
A nd cheering from the home
L aughing from my players as they
L ift the cup.

James Vaughan (10)
Stewart Fleming Primary School, Anerley

My Pet Sherman

My pet Sherman
Is grey with long ears
He is really long
And other cats he fears

My pet Sherman
Growls at dogs
He is really fierce
And he chases frogs

My pet Sherman
Is really lazy
He sleeps half the day
And sometimes he goes crazy

My pet Sherman
Has big eyes
He can run really fast
I hope he never dies
And he's a cat.

Mark Reddie (8)
Stewart Fleming Primary School, Anerley

Hair

Boring ponytail I think not
I've got loads of hair bands
So let's use the lot
Plaits and curls from funny worlds
Rainbow colours in my hair
Let's go crazy cos I don't care!

Faye Blamire (11)
Stewart Fleming Primary School, Anerley

My Dad's Eye

I know you've
Been through pain
I know you'll be
Normal again

It must be really
Painful in your eye
And when you went for your operation
It was hard to say bye

I know it is hurting you
And you're being strong
And I know for
Healing it's taking long

Please take it
Very, very slow
And it will heal
That's what I know.

Oghenevorke Kalusi Ejeta (11)
Stewart Fleming Primary School, Anerley

Winter

Winter is so nice because sometimes we see snow.
Winter is so nice because the winds strongly blow.
Winter is so nice because it is always cold and dark.
Winter is so nice because we walk to the park.
Winter is so nice because we have funny snowball fights.
Winter is so nice because of the lovely Christmas lights.
Winter is so nice because my class is always warm.
Winter is so nice because I can see icicles form.
Winter is so nice because I walk through the leaves.
Winter is so nice because of the red nose I achieve.

Jacob Jude Skelly (8)
Stewart Fleming Primary School, Anerley

World War II (Concentration Camp)

Imagine if you were there
Had to have blue eyes and blonde hair
You had to be really strong
And could not do anything wrong.

Imagine if you were there
Had to have blue eyes and blonde hair
You cried every single day
The Germans never went away.

Imagine if you were there
Had to have blue eyes and blonde hair
If you were a Jew it was a hard life
Living on the edge of a knife.

Imagine if you were there
Had to have blue eyes and blonde hair
You heard the sweet music coming from the train
But never realised you would end up in pain.

Amara Lalemi-Jacobs (10)
Stewart Fleming Primary School, Anerley

Freddie

There once was a boy called Freddie,
He had a big, fat belly,
He ate all the jelly,
And the fat covered the wide-screen telly.

He got taken out of school,
Because his belly filled up the hall,
He always got picked on,
And the next day he was gone.

Jordan Aaron Vidal (11)
Stewart Fleming Primary School, Anerley

How She Must Have Felt

(Based on Anne Frank arriving at the concentration camp)

Walking down the crusty stairs,
Hearing music in my ears,
Seeing trains go by and by,
'I want to go home,' I hear children cry.

Our train pulls up to a building so tall,
What is in store for me?
What's in store for us all?

I'm in the building,
It's ever so cold,
I hear people screaming,
I'm scared, oh no!

I want to go home,
I don't like it here,
Will I escape?
As I shake with fear.

Eloise Willis (11)
Stewart Fleming Primary School, Anerley

The Dreadful Singer

There once was a singer
Who went to a dinner
He drank all night
And he got into a fight.

He forgot that he had a show
And the audience was very low
He got sacked the very next day
And went far, far away.

Brandon Tuckey-Wood (11)
Stewart Fleming Primary School, Anerley

The Brave Boy

(This is based on a terrible accident to my brother Jamie Hillman's arm)

A tear from the eye,
A scream from the lips,
Blood from his arm,
Which tends to drip.

The sister screams,
The footsteps come,
His mind's so shocked,
He feels so numb.

The family cries,
Surprise, surprise,
But the brave boy,
No tears from his eyes.

The medicine runs through his veins,
And eventually he screams with pain,
But now he's back home,
And I'm massaging his scars,
I'm going to make a wish to the stars.

Thank You, God,
For my brother's life today,
So thank You, Lord,
I don't know what to say,
Accept I love him with all my heart,
And this is a beginning of a fresh new start.

Elizabeth Hillman (11)
Stewart Fleming Primary School, Anerley

Nightmare

There was an old man with grey hair
He went down to the new funfair
He went on the ghost train
And got a terrible pain
He woke up and it was all a nightmare.

George Phillips (11)
Stewart Fleming Primary School, Anerley

The Silly Poem

If you look closely you'll agree,
There are some silly sights to see.
Silly people passing by,
Have silly walks that you can try.
Silly ears, silly noses, silly necks,
And silly specs.
Silly beards, silly teeth,
Silly things worn underneath.
Silly hats are there to hide,
Some very silly heads inside!
And have you seen how odd it gets
When silly folk look like their pets?
Silly zebras, silly bears,
Silly sharks, silly hares.
My best friend, silly Ernie Klapp,
Built himself a mole trap.
The moles had made a bigger kind
And quickly caught him from behind.
Some silly people like to fly,
I've never known the reason why.
Babies eat some silly things
Like flies with wriggly legs and wings.
But grown-ups eat them just as well,
Like wriggly frogs and snails that smell.

Micaela Lauren Truman (9)
Stewart Fleming Primary School, Anerley

It Was So Quiet

It was so quiet I heard snowflakes drifting.
It was so quiet I heard air blowing.
It was so quiet I heard conkers hitting on the ground.
It was so quiet I heard people's footsteps.
It was so quiet I heard cars whooshing.
It was so quiet I heard a fly buzzing.

Tony Brinkhurst (7)
Stewart Fleming Primary School, Anerley

Untitled

The cold winter bites,
The snow falls white.
The sun shines bright,
Yet there is no warmth from its light.
The fire blazes high,
While people in their beds die.
For the cold winter bites.

The warmth of spring has come,
Flowers start to bloom.
Winter meets its doom,
The grey of the sky dies,
As the sun clears the sky.
Trees sprout their leaves,
And the new spring brings the bees.
For spring has come.

Sam Jackson (11)
Stewart Fleming Primary School, Anerley

A World Of Terror

On that dreadful day sixty years ago,
Many men fought and died,
They fought on sea and air,
And on land side by side.

The British, American and other countries,
Fought together with might,
They landed in France on D-Day,
And saw the Germans in sight.

After the fierce and dreadful battle,
We won with all our teams,
The field looked like a toxic wasteland,
And they still hear the terrible screams.

Jack Osmond (11)
Stewart Fleming Primary School, Anerley

Sports

Ball-kicker
Wicket-hitter
Bat-swinger
Footy-winger
Shot-saver
Party-beaver
Gavel-thrower
Thrown-lower
Rugby-catcher
Head-scratcher
Point-winner
Dart-pinner.

Melissa Caton (11)
Stewart Fleming Primary School, Anerley

Spring

S unflower buds sprouting out everywhere.
P ollen, strong smelling, so sweet and ripe.
R oses red, don't nod your head.
I love the blossom, pink and blue, it makes the world look nice.
N utritious nuts so sweet make me want to say, *'Bleep, bleep.'*
G ardens, gardens sprouting green,
I'll just sit there and want to dream.

Rephael Maloney (10)
Stewart Fleming Primary School, Anerley

Spring

S pring is a lovely time of year,
P opping out flowers come,
R ising up, going high,
I n spring it's a lovely time of year,
N ow you know what spring is like,
G o and look outside in the spring.

Alastair Park (9)
Stewart Fleming Primary School, Anerley

Kennings Cat

Fish-eater
Mouse-chaser
Little-racer
Mice-clearer
Dog-fearer
People-scratcher
Mouse-catcher
Whisker-flicker
Water-licker.

Ryan Kerbi (11)
Stewart Fleming Primary School, Anerley

Footballer

Ball-hitter
Goal-nicker
Red-devil
Gary Neville
Fast-runner
Next-gunner
Great-turner
Goal-saver.

Stephan Stewart (10)
Stewart Fleming Primary School, Anerley

Spring

S pring is the time when flowers bloom.
P utting a new life in place.
R eady to see beautiful colours.
I love spring.
N othing is bad about spring.
G etting ready to see the warm sunrise.

Hayley Urquhart (10)
Stewart Fleming Primary School, Anerley

Kennings Dog

Face licker
Tail wagger
Cat chaser
Bone cruncher
Ear flapper
Loud barker
Noisy snorer
Wet noser
People liker.

Ashleigh Walsh (11)
Stewart Fleming Primary School, Anerley

Dog

Face-licker
Tail-flicker
Bone-stealer
Bone-burier
Man-licker
Angry-biter
Scared-racer
Cat-chaser.

Petros Hajioannou (11)
Stewart Fleming Primary School, Anerley

A Winter's Night

A dark and stormy night,
Floor all fluffy and white.
Snowflakes falling to the ground,
Robins calling all around.
Fantastic snowball fights,
In the snowy, snowy nights.
Black crows calling all the time,
Snow always falling to the ground.

Ellie Hall (11)
Stewart Fleming Primary School, Anerley

A Penguin On Ice

The penguins stroll across the ice.
The warm sun rises
As the penguins' slippery gold and white skins reflect on the ice.
They scoot down the snowy, icy slopes
Their little fluffy babies shiver in the cold
Whilst their babies rest on their daddies' feet.
When the penguins slide in the sea
They go deep into the water.
The babies slide down too
So they don't get left behind
And die of starvation.
They live in the North Pole
Where it is cold
And they love it there.

Jill Stevenson (10)
Stewart Fleming Primary School, Anerley

I Am Afraid . . .

I am afraid of big, hairy tarantulas
Because they feel horrid and they are nasty creatures.
I am afraid of big heights
Because when I look down it feels like I'm going to fall
And crack my head open.
I am afraid of when I wake up
And there are horror movies on.
I am afraid of big grey sharks
Because if you are swimming in water
They could just come and gobble you up.
I am afraid of drowning when I go in the big blue sea
Because I might get washed away in the waves.
I am afraid of big, slippery snakes sliding across the floor.

Laurren Mitchell (8)
Stewart Fleming Primary School, Anerley

My Violin

Violin, where have you been?
Violin, where have you been all day long?
I've been practising my song
I want you so please come back.
You're supposed to be in my backpack
But oh no! You are not there.

I remember you were in Malcolm's room
But no, oh no!
You must be there
If not where can you be, violin?

I've been crying, crying every day
Now I remember it must be in my room
But no, but yes, hooray!
It is in my room!
Violin, lovely violin, playing sounds
Playing tunes every day,
Monday, Tuesday and Wednesday
Playing me tunes every day.

Bruno Telmo-Ponte (8)
Stockwell Primary School, Brixton

Snow

Snow is icing on your birthday cake.
Snow is a beautiful little cloud falling from the sky.
Snow is white dots on the ground.
Snow is a round sugar circle in your tea.
Snow is a big white ball rolling down the hills.
Snow is white marbles falling from Heaven.

Ramona Blackwood (10)
Stockwell Primary School, Brixton

Landscape In Front Of Me

I was running around on the beach,
Running with the wind,
When I stopped.
There, in front of me, was a mist,
And mountains.
I decided to climb up the mountains.
As I sat and looked ahead.
I could see, in front of me,
A landscape.
In front of me was a boat,
Not an ordinary boat,
A boat full of laughter.
I ran ahead to the boat,
And then when I tried to get inside it
There was nothing there.
It must have been a mirage.
It was all a dream,
The landscape in front of me.

Jennelle Reece-Gardner & Miranda (10)
Stockwell Primary School, Brixton

Riddle Poem

I am round like the sun,
I feel like a bun,
I am black and white,
I can go high as a kite,
I can charge like a bull.
What am I?

A football!

Mohammed Rahman (10)
Stockwell Primary School, Brixton

My Friend

Memories of you keep haunting me,
The places we met,
Just you and me.
The laughter and the fun we had,
How I wish I could have it all back.
If only I could turn back time,
Then everything would be just fine.
All I have are memories,
Which sometimes make me sad,
But sometimes when I think of you,
I am very glad.
Glad that I had a special friend,
Unfortunately it had to come to an end.
Perhaps one day we'll meet again,
If both of us end up in Heaven,
Well, that's what I intend.

Emranur Rahman (11)
Stockwell Primary School, Brixton

Fire

I am like an angry man,
My flames climb up
The burning house.
My favourite food is
Clothes, it makes me
More violent.
I am like Superman
With laser vision heating up
Your food.
I'm always dressed in
Red and orange, sometimes blue.
My worst enemy is water,
It kills me.

Sofia Spencer (11)
Stockwell Primary School, Brixton

Fire

I begin as a child
Growing faster and faster
Slapping people as I grow
Water I hate
For that is my fate
It would extinguish me once and for all
I bully all that I meet
Hurting each and every one
All the while
Though I try to smile
I burn and suffer
So I lash out at others
To take the pain away
Everyone tries to kill me
Bringing water to finish me
But I avoid it
For water is my angel of death
As soon as it touches me
I am no more
Yet as I grow old
With nothing to fuel me
Wishing that someone would give me wood
My life like a phoenix finishes
For I am now too weak to draw away
As at last they reach me
Splashing water upon me.

Hanan Mohamed (10)
Stockwell Primary School, Brixton

Football

Thursday is the day for football,
Sometimes Sundays too.
I play for one team now,
But I used to play for two.

I play for Seymour Villas,
And I think they're brill.
We went a team unbeaten,
The other team scored nil.

I won a trophy,
For playing very well.
Don't know why I won it though,
Because when I shot I fell.

I'm a defensive midfielder,
And I'm number nine.
And I've scored the most goals,
In the shortest time.

I went to trials at Kata Park,
At Kata Park,
The instructor said I was big and strong,
Like Noah's ark!

I support Arsenal,
So does Shem.
Arsenal beat Bromley,
By umm . . . ten!

Tesfa Atere (8)
Stockwell Primary School, Brixton

The Witch's Kitchen

All the witches in Witherland,
Love the food that Mandy makes.
Aliens visit and make snake desserts,
For all the witches in Witherland.

'Mmm,' says Mandy the witch,
Who has green and yellow-coloured hair.
People say, 'Boo!'
She says, 'Boo!' too.

Once she made sugar pongs,
With mice and spice,
With sugar lice,
Eyeballs and hair,
In one big pot.
'Mmm,' say all the witches,
In Witherland,
'We'll have this again.'

Janel Peddie (9)
Stockwell Primary School, Brixton

Best Friends

Best friends keep secrets
In their thoughtful heads
Never to tell a person, keep it instead.
I play with them every day
Never give a secret away
That's my best friends and that we'll always stay.

Nandipa Mukosi (8)
Stockwell Primary School, Brixton

Night Light

Can I have a night light?
Yes of course you can.
I'll put it on
The landing
To beat the bogeyman.

He doesn't like a bright light.
He doesn't like the glare.
It swallows up
The darkness
And shows he isn't there.

You can have a night light
Burning bright and strong
To drive away
The darkness
All night long.

Leon Cross (9)
Stockwell Primary School, Brixton

My Birthday Comes

My birthday comes with
Balloons flying
My birthday comes with
My friends laughing
My birthday comes with
A big cake inside writing
My birthday comes with
Presents like a kite flying
My birthday comes with
Cooking
My birthday comes with
Sweets like sugar
My birthday comes with . . .

Josselyn Jara Gonzaga (10)
Stockwell Primary School, Brixton

Fireball

I burn into flames,
I run as fast as I can,
The boiling water burns,
My head goes round,
My heart is pumping,
I look down over the Earth,
In the water of gain I see,
My hair scatters around me,
I hear the sound of hailstones,
My heart is pumping,
Not jumping,
I see a light,
I hear thunder,
I try changing directions,
I'm sliding left to right,
It's no use,
I swift away,
With no energy,
I am weak,
What can I do?

Blessing Oburoh (10)
Stockwell Primary School, Brixton

Ice Cream!

Ice cream is as white as snow!
Ice cream is tasty!
Ice cream is as nice as chocolate!
Ice cream is creamy!
Ice cream is like a dream!
Ice cream is smooth!
Ice cream is the nicest thing on Earth!
Ice cream smells like milkshakes!
Ice cream is nicer than sweets!
Oh how I love ice cream!

William Elliott (9)
Thomas's, Battersea

Whale

It lay upon the island's shore,
In the shallow nothing of an outgoing tide.
It struggled against acquainted weight,
Its lungs exhausted in raging heat.

People came and said, 'Kill it, it is just food.'
And the wise man said, 'It is sacred, it must not be harmed.'
A woman came with an empty shell,
And let it run silently over the whale's blue bulk.
The titanic stomach was flattened against sand
Like a face against a window.

The woman stayed, hour by hour, as the tide went out.
Breaths coming in harsh spasms.
It's slowly darkening in the burning sun.
The woman made girls from the village make a chain,
Pouring fresh water over the darkening blubber.

The whale didn't move as the moon came up.
The woman stroked his head, as she sang to him.
She sang of children grown and gone, and of people long dead.
She sang of passionate love.
Deep into the darkness,
When breaths almost lost touch,
She leant cheek to cheek with the whale.

Many stories dwelt in the moonlight then.
Her voice, with coaxing pauses,
Was as if it was bearing his to the surface of the ocean.
To look up, love and live.
With a tear of blood falling to the damp sand,
The whale let life slip,
To the raging sun.

Emma Irving (9)
Thomas's, Battersea

Broken Inside

I did not know the feelings she held,
The feelings she felt every day.
I could not help her,
Only watch her make the same mistakes again.
There were muscles on her body,
Strength, she had none.
She shed tears until there were no more to cry.
Her soul is broken.
She wants to go home,
She yearns to go home,
But if she went there would be no one to greet her.
She's lost in a world where people don't know how to help her,
If they could help her.
If I could help her.

She's shattered inside.

She hears no happiness,
She is deaf to love,
But her hearing is acute to wretched,
Mournful heartbroken sounds,
Ones I cannot describe.

Her eyes see only the ones in despair,
They convert a laughing being to a grovelling child,
Grief-stricken by the death of a loved one.

Her feelings she hides are undiscovered,
Never to be discovered.
She is all over the place,
She cannot find her place
And maybe never will.

She feels only the cold, the wet,
The harsh winds snapping at her face.

She's broken inside.

Emilie Cornelis (9)
Thomas's, Battersea

The Stream

A stream smells like a huge pile of pine cones
That are the sweetest and juiciest ever.

It sounds like birds chirping
With the sun's most wonderful song,

And it tastes like melted sugar
Rushing down your throat, desperate to get to the bottom.

A stream looks like the clearest crystal
Charging in a mighty flood.

It's the colour of sunbeams and moonbeams
Mixed together and poured into the world.

Its waters feel like the fur on the softest doe that ever lived.

A stream makes me think of midnight.

Kismet Bandeen (8)
Thomas's, Battersea

Summertime

Summer makes me feel cheerful and joyful,
It is the taste of freshly baked baguettes.
Summer is the sound of giggles and laughter filling the air.
It is the colour of rich ruby-red.
Summer is the scent of glistening flowers and the blazing hot sun.
Summer is the time when lambs bounce around
And children come out to play games on the juicy green fields.
I love summer!
Especially when I sunbathe on a hot summer's day!

Isabelle Scott (9)
Thomas's, Battersea

Eagle

I see the mystic eagle soaring through the air,
Its eyes glinting golden,
Both fixed in a stare.
Its claws are sharpened,
Its strengthened beak,
Its feathers glossy, smooth and sleek.

I hear its hunting call,
Piercing through the plains,
Marking its prey's fall,
Wounded in the rain.
Its wings pulsing, beating down,
Warning off prey for miles around.

In its presence I look meek,
Feeling humble, slightly weak.
As I think of its clawed feet,
I imagine the power of its lethal beak.

Maddie Bono (10)
Thomas's, Battersea

Thirst

Thirst is black like the monster in my cupboard.
It sounds like thousands of children begging for water.
It tastes like a bowl of sand with beetles inside.
It smells like an empty waterhole in Africa.
It looks like dried-up skeletons in a black cave.
It feels scratchy like crocodile's skin.
It reminds me of a hot day in an Indian desert.
Thirst is horrible.

Sofia Donavan (8)
Thomas's, Battersea

Second World War

I looked around and stared
At the people dying there
In the cold, dark world of death.
A huge flash in the sky
Then I wondered why
Why do people die over a man?

Suddenly a crash along with a flash
And everything flew in the air.
I screamed as my leg
Seemed to be dead
As I could not move it at all.

I started to yelp
And called for help.
Nobody came
Even though I was lame.
I don't know why
But I started to cry.

I tried to keep my life
Then go home to my wife
And have only bad memories.
Then I saw some folk
Starting to choke
As gas bombs filled the air.

Then I heard a *bang*
They had shot me in the head.
I was dead.

Claudia Gordon (10)
Thomas's, Battersea

My Hero

(My dad who has died)

His maths is better than a calculator.
Wow . . .
He's better than a monkey swinging from the trees.
Golly gosh . . .
His hair is grey as a rainy cloud
Oh . . .
He saves people from drowning.
His jokes are funnier than a clown's.
Well, nearly . . .
He's kinder than 1,000 stars in the sky.
He's hardworking too.
He had a medal from the Queen for raising funds.
Is that true?
He looks after nature, if you know what I mean.
Happy and jolly.
He's hopeful.
His face is as shining as a sun.
He's very friendly.
He's playful like a child laughing.
He's loving and caring.
He's generous and has a glowing face.
His eyes are like glass.
He travels a lot too.
He's sharing and buys everyone sweets.

I wish he was here . . .

Sophie Davies (8)
Thomas's, Battersea

Hunger

Hunger is white, blank-white, like the snow.
Hunger feels dry and painful.
Pain like when a sharp needle gets injected
Right into your cold, sour heart.
Hunger tastes like a bundle of cotton and tissue in your mouth.
Hunger smells like an empty, deep, dark cave
With leaking drops from the rain.
Hunger sounds like a sick, coughing person
Falling into a never-ending narrow hole.
Hunger feels like you even want to eat a pillow
Because you are so hungry.
Hunger reminds me of death.
Hunger is horrible.

Caroline Dreesmann (9)
Thomas's, Battersea

The Sound Of Silence

Have you heard a barn owl flying past?
Can you hear the plane cutting through the air
Or hear a spider spinning its web?
Have you heard your hair growing or falling?
Can you hear the seasons changing?
Have you heard the water freezing in winter
Or the world turning round?
Have you heard the electric car whizzing past?
Can you hear the sound of silence?

Can you?

Spencer Shapeero (8)
Thomas's, Battersea

Sound Of Silence

Have you heard a butterfly
Beating its wings
Or clouds changing to animals
So slowly, so silently?

Can you hear a rainbow
Painting itself in the sky
Or a paintbrush stroking across your page
So delicate, so quiet?

Have you heard an eye blinking
On someone's face
Or angels singing up in Heaven
So beautiful, so quiet?

Can you hear fish
Breathing in the water
Or the air blowing against you?

Can you hear them?

Alba Faggionato (8)
Thomas's, Battersea

The Sound Of Silence

Have you heard the sound of a dog's dream
So slow through the head?

Have you heard the sniff of a bird
So silent and lonely?

Have you heard the twitch of whiskers
So fast and lively?

Can you hear the air sliced by Concorde
So quick and quiet?

Can you hear the sounds of silence?

Jeremie Crystal (8)
Thomas's, Battersea

The Sound Of Silence

Can you hear your teeth cutting through the food
Or leaves falling off a tree in autumn
Or the birds flying in the sky?

Can you hear the sun rising up
Or the sooty ink all over the page
Or your nails growing?

Can you hear a bumblebee making honey in the flowers
Or looking at something
Or a window watching outside?

Can you hear your bones growing
Or the clouds starting to get angry
Or a rainbow about to rise?

Can you hear a snake sliding around
Or plants growing
Or freckles growing on cheeks?

Ortensia Fioravanti (8)
Thomas's, Battersea

The Leopard

Flopped in a tree I see a leopard.
Its solid black spots disguising itself.
Its glinting eyes surveying the plain.
It freezes.
It relocates to the long grass carpet.
It begins to stalk with frozen concentration.
Bouncing shoulders along the emerald plain.
It tiptoes towards its prey.
It starts its charge with anticipation.
A fatal bite at the neck confirms its victory.

Rosanna Beart (9)
Thomas's, Battersea

The Shark

The mystical killer glides silently through the deep blue
And seemingly ever-still waters.
Searching intently; his wicked eye glinting in the murky waters.
His head snaps back!
He has seen his hunted and is now the hunter.
At the edge of his vision the prey swims on
Unconscious of the large predator.
Here it comes!
He swims fast, he speeds.
The mighty shark shoots forward,
An immense biting torpedo with infinite teeth, arched back
And a grin splashed on his face.
He sweeps over his prey,
Bloodshot eyes peering down,
Opens his mouth and pauses;
Two tiny figures move, blotches in the dark.
He pauses again.
The mighty warrior strikes and then carries his prize away,
Leaving the other to swim away,
Followed by a cloud of blood.

Humphrey Galbraith (10)
Thomas's, Battersea

The Wolf's Attack

The wolf's footsteps whisper through the forest.
Suddenly his eyes fall onto a snow-white fluff ball.
His piercing teeth glint in the moonlight.
Suddenly he goes for his attack but the rabbit springs out.
Annoyed, the wolf turns and disappears into the distance,
Leaving his howl mixing into the midnight air.

Arabella Dear (9)
Thomas's, Battersea

I Spy A Shark!

The shark is watching slyly through the reeds for its prey.
It slices through the water, cutting it to pieces.
He is blue-washed from his head to his fin,
A speedboat full of razors,
Spinning like a propeller, it glides through the water.
Sharp, slippy skin glistening in the sea's light.
Quiet, silent, not making a noise,
Swishing with his fin, pushing through the sea floor jungle.
The murky water hides his glinting smile of yellow teeth.
A dark shadow creeps along the sea floor,
It plunges down deeper into the aqua depths.
He searches for his prey and spots it.
The shark licks his lips; now he is the predator.
The shark's eyes glow red then it slowly opens its mouth.
The prey tries to make an escape but the shark is too quick.
With a snap of his jaws he's swallowed up his unsuspecting prey
And disappears back into the reeds, watching once more.

Ned Botwood Smith (9)
Thomas's, Battersea

The Cobra

I lay there, stunned by the heat,
But then my eyes caught a smudge of brown
In the long, lashing grass.
I uncoiled my scaly body and went to get a better hunter's view.
It was a field mouse munching a berry.
I slithered forward until I was a metre away.
I drew in my breath and I pounced and caught it by the tail.
It was pulling like a dog on a leash.
I swallowed before someone saw my smirk.
I glided away to find more food.

Poppy Ogier (10)
Thomas's, Battersea

I See A Mongoose

I see a mongoose
Slyly walking through the grass.
His silky straight skin brushing against the jungle carpet.
Then suddenly he stops
And looks around.
He sees a silent and shaking flamingo having a drink.
He carefully creeps towards the silent prey,
Always looking for deadly danger.
He gets ever closer, his heart beating like a drum.
Then he stops!
He waits, as silent as the dead, to make his move.
He gets ready to pounce like a coiled spring.
He attacks!
He springs into the air like a violent viper,
Catching his prey and shredding it to pieces like a lion in his den.
He drags it off into the murky darkness of the jungle carpet.

Max Burt (10)
Thomas's, Battersea

The Sound Of Silence

Have you heard the sound of the seasons changing
Or a calculator calculating?

Have you heard the sound of a fly flying
Or your hair growing?

Have you heard the wind changing
Or a bird soaring in the blue sky?

Have you heard the sound of the bedroom window frosting
Or your best friend's thoughts?

Have you heard the sound of a lake turning to brittle ice
Or a tropical orchard swaying in the breeze?

Have you heard?

Alice Anderson (9)
Thomas's, Battersea

A Cheetah

A cheetah lurked in the shade of the tree,
It clambered down the maroon tree trunk.
The cheetah had spotted an antelope.
Its eyes glinted.
It had a coat made of gold.
The cheetah quivered with excitement.
It stalked through the emerald grass.,
The animal's mouth was watering with hunger.
It was catching up speed.
The cheetah was running like a bolt of lightning
Being struck on a dark night.
A strike of fear hit the antelope
But the cheetah's mission had been destroyed.

Daisy Agnew (9)
Thomas's, Battersea

The Cheetah

The cheetah's golden coat with
Chocolate spots dazzled in the
Morning sun.
He sped across the emerald fields
And there it was - lying in front
Of his eyes:
The antelope with no idea of
The danger that lay ahead.
He sneaked up on the innocent
Creature.
He paused, ready to pounce.
He pulled back and then
Leapt forward.
As he left, a trace of blood
Trailed after him.

Katherine Allan (10)
Thomas's, Battersea

The Sound Of Silence

Can you hear the sound of a mouse scuttling across the floor
Or can you hear the clock ticking from next door?

Have you heard snakes shedding their skin
Or can you hear memories flowing through your ear?

Can you hear words being let into your mind
Or can you hear a rainbow being arced into the sky?

Have you heard a person rubbing cream into their skin
Or have you heard a girl stretching her skirt?

Can you hear spirits being let into the sky
Or can you hear a dog sleep in its kennel?

Have you heard the snow falling from the sky
Or can you hear the grass growing old?

These are the sounds of silence.

Letitia Harkness (8)
Thomas's, Battersea

The Snake

The gleaming snake spots its prey,
Its skin bullet-proof.
Sliding over grass leaving a trail of venom behind.
Its hiss is noiseless, it hides away.
It coils around a rock, ready to pounce.
It glints in the glimmering sun.
Its teeth are razors as strong as steel.
It digs through the ground.
It snaps its mouth full of delight.
It scatters off into the woods.

Zachary Hobbs (10)
Thomas's, Battersea

Seasons

As the seasons come and go,
There's a tingling feeling in your toes,
Summer is sizzling hot,
Waves crashing against the rocks,
Don't forget about summer days,
Even though there are more to come,
Like autumn when leaves fall to the ground,
So many colours of the sun,
But remember winter when icy snowflakes rule the sky,
And all those days with your friends,
You made snowmen for days on end,
There's still another season, this, of course, is spring!
When daffodils are blooming all around your door,
A yellow carpet covering the floor,
So these are all the seasons.
Which one do you like best?
Whatever your choice - remember the rest!

Ela Stopford Sackville (9)
Thomas's, Battersea

The Eagle

The eagle, thin and gaunt, posing on a mountainside.
Searching, searching
For a flicker of life on the deserted landscape.
There, a movement, there it is.
Off he goes, air flying through his dappled coat,
Plummeting into the depths.
He pauses but only to sight his prey again.
Like an arrow he shoots towards the vulnerable field mouse.
He skims across the green turf.
He strikes and swoops into the blue-washed sky,
A limp body hanging from his bloodstained feet.

Charlotte Enoch (9)
Thomas's, Battersea

The Leopard

The sound lingered in my ear,
A sound of guns, my worst fear.
The poacher's triumphant cry filled the sky,
The injured leopard limped by.
A mother deprived of her child,
Her pride was hurt, no longer wild.
The poacher's grin only grew wider,
She had fallen into his web, a helpless fly, he was the spider.
As he loaded his gun,
She scampered off into the sun.
The vehicle started moving,
A tree stood in his way, looming.
The poacher was lost within the bush,
He gave the termites' mound a push.
He was mistaken, the mound came alive!
A leopard's roar came from inside.
The leopard was prowling, the poacher his prey.
He now knew not to stray.
The leopard pounced,
The poacher flinched.
His path was barred with drooling jaws,
He lay dead on the bush veldt's cruel floors.

Deia Tollman (10)
Thomas's, Battersea

The Sound Of Silence

Can you hear a ghost staring at you,
Or a monster swallowing spiky stones?

Can you hear a witch gliding on a broomstick,
Or a zombie tiptoeing to catch you?

Can you hear a mummy quietly making its way out of a cage,
Or a villain's mouth opening?

Cyrus Kamshad (9)
Thomas's, Battersea

Stag

His beady eyes focused on the moss
Whilst he proudly held his antlers high.
The daffodils whispered behind his back,
As he trudged along like a tramp
Not noticing the jewel-like apples hanging from the trees.
He lifted his hooves gloomily,
Which were like two stones fused together.
The wet moss of his coat surrounding his body
Suddenly became tense.
He spotted a gun glinting in the shadows.
Before all the blood was drained out of his face
He fell to the ground
Uttering his last words.
Lifeless as a desert.

Olivia Vickers (9)
Thomas's, Battersea

Fishing

The fishes swam around the lake
But they were doomed upon my wake.
The ducks went *quackity-quack*
And the wind made the reeds crack.
I was fishing for trout
That was what my life was all about.
That lovely breeze on my face
It was so gentle it would tie your shoelace.
I had my lunch and went back to the pond
Then one of the fish got caught on the frond.
It was quite big but also quite tall
Then again it was actually small.
At the end of the day it was really quite fun
When I got home my nose had begun to run.

Jonathan Richmond (10)
Thomas's, Battersea

Snow

The warmth inside,
I feel deprived.
Alone outside.

As the morning sun shines down,
I jump around.
I feel like a clown!

The cold etches its way along my face,
Socks and shoes are all I wear.
I feel alone in an open space.

I wish I could fish,
Then cook over an open fire.
This is my only wish.

It is time to go,
I feel the fun drain from me.
I wish it wasn't so.

Ben Levinson (9)
Thomas's, Battersea

Friends

Friends are fun, they shine in the sun
Friends are cool, they always play pool

Friends are helpful, friends are thoughtful
Friends share, they always care
Friends are kind, they always mind

You can talk to your friends
But be careful
They sometimes talk nonsense!

Francesca Cattaneo (7)
Thomas's, Battersea

Sharks

Sharks slide and glide through the water,
They eat humans.
Sharks strike with accuracy,
Sharks like fish, they are big.
Sharks can smell blood a mile away,
They are black and grey.
They have rough skin,
Their teeth are as sharp as a pin.
They munch up their lunch,
It sounds like this - *crunch! Crunch!*
They kick with their fins and are curious about ships.
Blood attracts sharks,
Each time they eat,
They lose some teeth.
Sharks are fast,
They also lived in the past.

Patrik Andersen (8)
Thomas's, Battersea

The Beach

I can hear the waves ripple and crash down.
I can feel the burning sand on my feet.
I can see the sandcastles in front of me.
I can hear the birds' wings flap.
I can feel the water touch my toes.
I can see the waves roll forward.
I can hear all the children splashing in the water.
I can feel the cool air blowing on my face.
I can see the blue clouds above me.
I can hear people playing with beach balls.
I can feel the sand blowing in the air on the beach.

Matthew Main (10)
Thomas's, Battersea

The Sound Of Silence

Have you heard a plane
Cutting through the clouds,
A bird crying
For its mum?

Can you hear water
Falling into a person's mouth,
So crisp, so silent?

Have you heard a hand
Waving in the air,
A foot wriggling
In a shoe?

Can you hear a rabbit weeping,
A spider weaving silk,
So gentle, so quiet?

Have you heard years passing,
Rain freezing,
Snow falling?

These are the sounds of silence.

Charlotte Hull-Sieff (9)
Thomas's, Battersea

The Beach

The beach's golden sun makes you so jolly inside.
The cyan waves of the sea
And clouds of fish surrounding the water black and gold.
The ginger sand hurts your eyes.
The navy sea surrounds the land.
The white horses of waves turn you over.

Nicolas Cornelis (7)
Thomas's, Battersea

The Sound Of Silence

Can you hear a rubber,
A rubber rubbing out a word?
Can you hear a fish,
A fish breathing for air?

Can you hear a ghost,
A ghost striking you dead
Or a snake,
A snake shedding its skin?

Can you hear somebody write
With pitch-black ink
Or a thought,
Somebody dreaming?

Can you hear a bird
Glide through the sky
Or a cheetah
Speeding through a forest?

These are the sounds of silence.

Val Ismaili (8)
Thomas's, Battersea

On A Hot Summer's Day

I feel the sun scorching my neck.
I feel the grass graze my legs.
I feel the air whipping my face.
I see the trees blossoming under the care of the sun.
I see the grass shrivel in the heat.
I hear the birds chirping in the tree.
I hear the waving of the tree leaves.
I hear the scampering of the fox.
I feel the welcoming warmth of the sun.
I see the superior light of the sun.
I hear nature's creations on a hot summer's day.

Antoine Grey (9)
Thomas's, Battersea

Summer's Day

I can see the raging sea.
I can see the beautiful blue sky.
I can see the mad children running about in the sand.
I can see big ships in the distance.
I can see the beach houses ready to be used.
I can hear the waves crashing against the shore.
I can hear the seagulls twittering in the background.
I can hear the children screaming with joy.
I can hear cars pulling in to have fun at the beach.
I can hear people having fun in the sea.
I can hear the strong wind making a whistling noise.
I can hear children scraping the sand out of the ground.
I can hear the stones clattering in the children's buckets.
I can smell the sea air.
I can smell the hot sand.
I can smell the exhaust of the cars' fumes.
I can smell the wood of the beach huts.
I can feel the hot sand on my back.
I can feel the sun burning my skin.
I can feel the cold sea on my feet.

Max Holland (10)
Thomas's, Battersea

The Car Shop

It smells so new,
It looks so cool,
The car shop, I stick to it like glue.
The cars so clean,
The cars so bright,
I dream of cars and cars all night!
I don't count sheep, I count cars,
I dream of Golfs - the size of Mars!
The car shop, the place to hitch a ride,
Too bad I've never been inside!

Jake Morgan (9)
Thomas's, Battersea

Seal's Lunch

Gliding through the crystal waters,
Swooping in-between the dazzling coral,
Shimmers of light dancing across your back,
Chasing and playing, chasing and playing.
Tropical seas lap against your stony-grey, curious face.
Diving deep into inky-black waters,
Plummeting down, plummeting down.
The shrill call of the rainbowfish
Reminds you that lunch is escaping.
Strands of seaweed brush across your slender body.
A sense of excitement grips you.
With a sudden jolt of speed you dart forward
And catch it between your silky paws, silky paws.
A wave of shock spreads through your body.
A great dark beast is circling you.
You dash away to shallow waters.
The dreaded shark with rocky eyes and thorny teeth is gone.
You swim back to shore.
A herald of barking seal pups awaits you.
But this does not stop you slipping back
Into a world of dreams and happiness . . .

Charles Campbell (9)
Thomas's, Battersea

Sweets!

S nake sweets, slimy sweets, all types of sour sweets!
W arm sweets, wiggly sweets, all types of wonky sweets!
E lephant sweets, elf sweets, all types of energy sweets!
E vil sweets, enormous sweets, all types of enjoyable sweets!
T rumpet sweets, terrifying sweets, all types of tempting sweets!
S ilvery sweets, slippery sweets, all types of sickly sweets!

Kate Sullivan (8)
Thomas's, Battersea

The Fire Of London

Houses crackling, soon to be ash,
Valuable goods turning to worthless trash.
People screaming, jumping into the filthy river.
A little child running to her helpless mother
And giving a little shiver.
Swooshes of brown water blanketing the fiery blaze,
Many tearstained-faced families sadly gaze.

The swoosh of filthy water covering the fire,
Birds flying away and falling.
People rowing in the Thames,
A teenage girl jumps in the river and shouts, 'Run Emms!'
A large strip of fiery wood plunges into the water.
'Is the water cold?' someone asks.
'Sorta.'

Everything ever owned is gone.
Wrecked is the lawn.
The dog is dead,
He was burnt on the head.
Everything is helpless, we can do nothing at all.
Everyone will fall.

Witt Kegel (9)
Thomas's, Battersea

I Prefer Dogs

I prefer dogs.
Dogs chase cats and try to leap on them,
Cats are fast runners so dogs always miss.
Dogs are cosy with their brown furry bodies,
Cats can be vicious with their sharp claws.
Dogs love their tummies being tickled,
Cats have scratchy fur.
I prefer dogs.

Alexander Galbraith (8)
Thomas's, Battersea

The Minotaur

His teeth are razor-sharp
His blood, scarlet-red.
His eyes are nearly dead,
His body is flooded with blood.
His muscles are strained and bulging,
His horns are blunt and cracked.
He smells blood and hears a thud.
He runs for his prey.
He grunts.
The prey's sword glimmers in the light.
They both groan.
The prey throws a stone
And then . . . stabs the beast with the glimmering sword.
Blood flows out.
The beast is dead . . .

Tom Veljanovski (9)
Thomas's, Battersea

The Sound Of Silence

Have you ever heard a pen writing,
Or a caterpillar laying its eggs?
Have you ever heard a tree growing,
Or a rainbow slowly fading away?
Have you ever heard a person reading,
Or a squirrel eating nuts?

Have you ever heard a boy sleeping,
Or a season changing?
Have you ever heard a teacher getting ready to yell,
Or a fly walking up the wall?
Have you ever heard a boy blinking?

Can you hear?

Alexander Aldridge (9)
Thomas's, Battersea

My Baby Brother

My brother is very small.
He weighs about ten pounds.
He has tiny ears, no teeth and a little bit of hair.
My little brother is called Will.
He cries a bit, not a lot.
He has tiny feet.
He is sick a bit.
He sleeps loads.
My brother has short arms.
His skin is smooth.
He has a small nose.
He only drinks milk.
The back of his head can fit in my hand.
He wears nappies.
He doesn't have very much hair.
I can't wait until he grows up.
He will be really fun.

George Thomas (8)
Thomas's, Battersea

Toffee, The Horse

Toffee has a velvet, brown, chestnut coat,
Toffee has blue eyes
Like the ocean waves lapping against the golden sand.
Toffee has a rough nose like sandpaper,
Toffee has silky hair
Like a princess' black locks swaying in the wind.
Toffee has a wild mind like a huge wind racing through a jungle,
Toffee is as sweet as the sugar lumps you hold in your hand.
Toffee has a heart you can hold,
Toffee has a heart of gold.

Emily Scott (7)
Thomas's, Battersea

The Sound Of Silence

Can you hear the days go by,
Or the starfish breathing
In the round rock pool?
No, these are silent sounds.

Have you heard your hair growing,
Or my pen
Writing across the blank page?
No, these are silent sounds.

Can you hear a bird flying,
Or a rainbow forming
In the blue sky?
No, these are silent sounds.

Have you heard your eye blinking,
Or the water freezing
Crystal and smooth?
No, these are silent sounds.

Can you hear the air blowing,
Or the world groaning
In the peaceful universe?
No, these are silent sounds.

These are sounds none will hear.

Madeleine Lacaille (8)
Thomas's, Battersea

Hate

I am as old as the midnight sky
I live in a piercing black hole in your heart
I make happiness come to an end
I love the sound of abominable bells
I loathe happiness ringing around and around
I love it when people have a row
I am hate.

Emma Pendrill (9)
Thomas's, Battersea

Can You Hear?

Can you hear the day
Awakening in the bright morning?
Can you hear the wind
Whispering its secrets?
Can you hear the fish
Fiddling and fluttering in the water?
I can.

Can you hear the clouds
Spluttering and spitting out the slippery sleet?
Can you hear the family
Nipping through their breakfast?
Can you hear the plates
Swiping clean away?
I can.

Can you hear the school bus
Parking at each house?
Can you hear the trees
Rustling in the clear wind?
Can you hear the night
Clearing the day for a new beginning?
Can you?

Alexander Mansfield (9)
Thomas's, Battersea

What Am I?

I last for however long the gold shining stars are in the moonlit sky.
I live on a red rose in the bottom of people's hearts.
I'm happy when two rightful human beings
Are enjoying their love life.
I feel proud when I see two people happy and joyful.

I am Love.

Nadja Orwell (9)
Thomas's, Battersea

Keep On Running . . .

(Written after reading 'Reynard The Fox' by John Masefield)

My heart beating,
Rapidly panting,
Tiredness growing,
Keep on running . . .

My tail drooping,
Savage hounds chasing,
Sweat dripping,
Keep on running . . .

My hopes rising,
My speed gaining,
Slightly grinning,
Keep on running . . .

My earth blocked,
Hopes dropped,
Heart stopped,
Keep on running . . .

Rupi Henderson (10)
Thomas's, Battersea

Everything

E lderberries, emus, elephants and eggs
V ixens, vacations, violets and violins
E levators, emerald, espresso and e-mail
R accoons, roses, rubies and ribs
Y o-yos, yoghurts, yawns and yoga
T urtles, TVs, turnips and tulips
H airstyles, headphones, hedgehogs and halos
I gloos, iguanas, indexes and inches
N apkins, needles, nests and nuts
G iraffes, gooseberries, grandparents and gyms.

Julia Quirk (10)
Thomas's, Battersea

The Attic

I'm up in the attic,
I see mice scampering around,
I travel around searching for a toy,
And I start to enjoy,
For I found a box,
That looked like a fox,
The gloomy figures I saw,
Looked a little raw,
I journeyed in the dark, cold place,
It looked a bit like outer space,
A smell drifted through the air,
Then I saw my toy mare,
I picked it up and had one big glare,
I started to stare,
Time had flown,
So I went back through the dark, old and cold.

India Dearlove (9)
Thomas's, Battersea

What Is Blue?

Blue is the raging sea in stormy weather.
Blue is the calm sea when the weather is gentle.
Blue is the clear sky with no clouds.
Blue is the graceful whales making loud noises in the ocean.
Blue and yellow make green, blue and red make purple.
When you feel blue you feel sad
And tears trickle down your cheeks.
I have blue eyes, some people do too.
When fire goes really hot it turns blue.
I hope you see how important blue is
Because I do.

Lucy Touche (7)
Thomas's, Battersea

Imagine . . .

Imagine being a dolphin soaring through the billowing sea,
Imagine going to an exhilarating funfair,
Candyfloss stalls all for me!

Imagine strolling through a field full of vibrant, fresh flowers,
Imagine if a fairy could grant your wishes throughout the hours!

Imagine if you could fly over a rainbow in a jumbo jet,
Imagine that you went to a casino and you win all your bets!

Imagine that you could fly up to Heaven
And meet all your ancestors.

Imagine!

Eliza Lorimer (9)
Thomas's, Battersea

I Am . . .

I am as old as the twinkling stars above,
Until they twinkle no more.
I live at the bottom of your heart
Where bad things are kept.
Nothing makes me happy
Except to see people fight.
I turn children's good dreams
To bad dreams.
I am afraid of turning into something
That loves and cares.
I am proud to see people screaming
In a piercing, high-pitched voice.

I am Hate.

Amadea Kimmins (10)
Thomas's, Battersea

The Sound Of Silence

Have you heard the world turning,
Steadily, as slow as can be,
Or a rainbow appearing,
Shining and glistening in the sun?

Have you heard the trees,
Whispering secrets as quiet as can be,
Or ladybirds,
Munching up aphids on a leaf?

Have you heard an eye blink,
Shimmering as pretty as can be,
Or your skin,
Peeling when you've been in the sun?

Have you heard a pin,
Drop on the carpet as silent as can be,
Or someone reading in their head,
Thinking of a land in their dreams?

I can,
In my thoughts.

Christina Trigle (9)
Thomas's, Battersea

My Dog

I have the *best* dog ever
She's got fur as black as the darkest of all night skies
And she's ever so clever
She makes my bed and cheers me up when I cry
And my dog even once spelt 'never'!
My dog is great because she makes me *pie!*
You see my dog is the best dog ever
Because she'll never ever die!

Only one thing - I wish my dog was real!

Madeleine Thirsk (9)
Thomas's, Battersea

The Sound Of Silence

Have you heard . . .

Have you heard a spider
Spinning a silky web,
Or a boy
Enjoying his book?

Have you heard the air
Swirling around the room,
Or a pen
Writing across the page?

Have you heard the water
Slowly freezing in the pool,
Or your hair
Growing around your head?

Have you heard a plane
Cutting through the sky,
Or your thoughts
Circling around your brain?

Have you heard a fly
Tapping against the wall,
Or the world
Growing older and older?

Have you heard the seasons
Switching from one to another,
Or a rainbow
Appearing in the blue sky?

Have you heard the years
Slowly passing by,
Or an eye
Blinking like lightning?

Tobias Murray (9)
Thomas's, Battersea

Sound Of Silence

Can you hear the air,
Brushing against the window,
So silent, so gloomy?

Have you heard the ink pen,
Flowing on a piece of paper,
So dull, so restless?

Can you hear cheeks blushing,
While watching horses graze,
So calm, so quiet?

Have you heard the rainbow,
Forming its colours,
So delightful, so colourful?

Can you hear the snow,
Falling on a tree,
So chilly, so bitter?

Have you heard the water,
Freezing in a fridge,
So nippy, so icy?

Can you hear the clouds,
Giving the land rain,
So grey, so sunless?

Only God can hear these sounds.

Georgina West (8)
Thomas's, Battersea

The Soldier

The soldier was crawling home from war
Staring at the dusty floor
He looked ahead with triumph
And then at his losses from war
Then back at the dusty floor
The soldier was crawling home from war.

Kyra Schulman (9)
Thomas's, Battersea

The Hunt

(Written after reading 'Reynard The Fox' by John Masefield)

As we ride . . . through the mist
And the hunting horns blow
The fox runs and twists
To a cry of a crow

As we ride . . . to hounds
The horses get slower
The fox goes to ground
Horses' heads fall lower

The fox is alone
The huntsmen retire
Sadly to home
And brandy and fire.

George Parry (10)
Thomas's, Battersea

World Of Clockwise

The clock ticks.
You stare at it
And all of a sudden
You fall in a daze.
You feel all dizzy.
All you see is a blaze,
A blaze of fire round and round,
Clockwise, never to stop.
The world is spinning,
Fast and clockwise,
Like an owl,
Spinning its head.
Your vision is blurry,
Your head is whirly.
Clockwise has countered!

Tom Stafford (10)
Thomas's, Battersea

My Heroine Josephine

She has long brown hair that is tied back in a bun
She is part of my life
Like a petal on a flower
She is ten years old
But as young as she feels
She is better at ballet than Darcy Bussell
She helps me every second I need her
She loves me dearly with all her heart
She is kind and thoughtful
(. . . but sometimes annoying!)
Oh! and so generous.
She is careful and full of joy!

Helena Benthall (8)
Thomas's, Battersea

Homework

Oh homework, oh homework, I wish you didn't exist.
You hurt my eyes when I look at you!
Your colours are grey and black, spooky too.
Oh homework, oh homework, I hate you, I really do.
You taste like rotten eggs on stinky bread!
You feel so slimy like snails' slime!
Oh homework, oh homework, you're crumply and so flat.
You remind me of the bad things that happened in school.
You sound like the teacher screaming behind me.
I wish I could burn you up and throw you away.
Who invented homework?
Whoever did, I'm not their best friend!

Xenia von Planta (8)
Thomas's, Battersea

Life Is . . .

(Written after reading 'Reynard The Fox' by John Masefield)

Running fast
Hounds behind
Coming last,
'Help!' I whined!
Life is waiting.

Heart thumping
Hope decreasing
Still panting
Keep running!
Life is sinking.

Thicker and thicker the mud gets
Harder and harder I see the nets
Faster and faster my feet run
More and more I hear the gun!
Life is waiting.

Death is behind me
My earth is in sight
The gun has been shot
It gave me a fright!

Everything still
Huntsman will kill
Earth is stopped!
Life is blocked!

Matilda Ellis (9)
Thomas's, Battersea

The Mad Café

Waiter, waiter,
There's an alligator
With a calculator
In my soup.
He's getting out of control now,
He's raising up his eyebrow,
He seems to be doing a dance,
He's getting up to prance.
Oh no, a snake's crawling up my back,
He's carrying a sack.
I don't know what to do,
Now he's turned into a kangaroo.
What a mad café!

Isabella Speaight (10)
Thomas's, Battersea

Babies

Babies always cry,
They sleepily lie.
Babies are sweet,
They have tiny feet.
Babies sneeze,
They're like a cool breeze.
They have different names:
Alexander, Bill and James.
'Mummy' and 'Daddy' are their first words,
Babies mostly like birds.
Their cries echo,
But they're scared of geckos!
They would like to sleep
With soft sheep.

Hugo Thomas (8)
Thomas's, Battersea

Friends

Friends are helpful, friends are your mates,
Friends are friendly and they share cakes.
Friends make you laugh, friends are fun,
Friends make you smile
And best of all
Friends keep you happy for a while.

Sasha Holland (8)
Thomas's, Battersea

The Haunted House

At once he got there and opened the door,
He looked round and said, 'Are you sure?'
Rob approached the bend and peered round,
He heard a funny kind of screeching sound.

It was beginning to sound like a laugh,
Rob is dumb, he thought it was a giraffe.
It was a witch who had lots of hair,
The nasty man is our mayor.

He walked into a dusty, cobwebbed room,
Rob saw a ghoul in the depths of the gloom!
Noises went *clash, clatter and boom . . . bang!*
The door slammed, a vampire viewed its fang.

'Check one, check two, what are you gonna do?'
'Wait five minutes while I go to the loo!'
Rob thought it was a good amusement park,
Dare you enter the haunted house?
This is where the monsters lark!

David Servant (10)
Thorntree Primary School, Charlton

Sunset Sea

The sea is shimmering light,
It is an overflowed puddle,
With underwater sea creatures,
And boats surf across the sea.

The sand is crushed-up rocks,
With seashells and pebbles washed upon it,
Making sandcastles and little streams,
Your feet just soak into the sand.

The sunset makes a colourful sky,
As people say it is shepherd's delight,
When it's summer it goes down late,
And when it's winter it goes down early.

The seagulls search for fish,
They dive in the water to catch them,
The birds glide across the sky,
The seagulls will fly beyond the sunset sea.

Nicole Miners (11)
Thorntree Primary School, Charlton

The Devil's Verse

Fear is the liquor of Hell
Hate is in the Devil's eyes
Sadness is the happiness of Satan
Loathing is the love of all things evil
Addiction is evil's intrigue of intoxication
Temptation is the apple of the Underworld
Anger is the helix of Hades
Wickedness is the way to eternal punishment
Cruelty is the core of the Neverworld
Sinning is the laws of the lower regions
Homicide is your one-way ticket to Hell
Suicide is where bliss is never found
Herbicide is punished with a joyless afterlife
The blood of a holy man is sick in Satan's eyes.

Josiah Adojutelegan (10)
Thorntree Primary School, Charlton

The Wacky Man

When the day was just dawning,
And the wacky man was yawning,
He strolled down the road very slow,
And met his biggest foe.

His foe had a machine gun,
And he hit him in the thumb,
He was gushing out with blood,
And he almost made a flood.

He started to prepare,
For the next day ahead,
He prepared a dangerous machine,
And it was fabulously clean.

When he saw his foe the next day,
He chased him right away,
The wacky man stopped there,
And shot his foe's house into the air.

Jake Hearnden (11)
Thorntree Primary School, Charlton

Colours Of Feelings

Happiness is yellow
Like the sunshine glistening
Sadness is blue
Like a deep well,
Pain is grey
Like a cloudy day,
Anger is red
Like an erupting volcano,
Hate is black
Like the dark night sky
But love has no colour,
It is something that gives you
A warm feeling in your heart.

Francesca Latamsing (10)
Thorntree Primary School, Charlton

The Six Senses

Fear is black, so dark and strong,
People fear snakes, spiders, the black widow's song.

Sadness is blue, so deep and slow,
It stays with you forever, doesn't leave your side.

Anger is red, so long and huge,
Sometimes with a person, maybe not, you choose.

Hate is orange, so fiery and meaningful,
So strong in a way you cannot name.

Happiness is golden, so bright and shimmery,
Like a beam of light straight from the sun.

Now it is time for the deepest of all,
So powerful you can't name it at all.
Love, it has no colour, it has no frame,
Love, it's something you cannot tame.

Holly Spencer (10)
Thorntree Primary School, Charlton

Natural Feelings

Anger is deep red like a blazing fire in a dark room.
Fear is black like an extremely dark cave.
Sadness is dark blue like a dark, stormy night.
Pain is deep purple like a newly-inflicted bruise.
Silence is blank like a plain piece of paper.
Happiness is colourful like a rainbow showering over the world.
Hate is deep orange building up in your body.
Hunger is light blue like a vegetable garden locked up.
Tiredness is grey like a bed waiting to be slept in.
Love is nothing, something so powerful you cannot describe,
Something that is stored in your heart.
These are a display of senses that you cannot control.

Ben Khoshnevisan (9)
Thorntree Primary School, Charlton

Happiness Is . . .

Happiness is golden
Like finding a friend,
Love is a rainbow
Like a person you never want to let go of,
Anger is red
Like losing that friend to somebody else,
Sadness is blue
Like sitting and knowing you can't get them back,
Curiosity is yellow
Like the house that you see as you sit in your pain,
Fear is black
Like what you see as you open the door of the house,
Pain is silver
Like dying and knowing you won't see them again,
Silence is white
Like death as you lie there alone,
Never to see or breathe again.

Sorren Alsford (9)
Thorntree Primary School, Charlton

Happiness

Happiness is golden, as gold as the sun, as gold as anything.
Happiness is full of fun and joy and laughter,
It never stops and never fades.
Happiness takes away pain,
Keeps you joyful and is always there to help.
Happiness never ends,
It lasts till the very end, even when you're dead.
Happiness is a force that never stops,
Never fades away, it's with you all the time,
When you're dead and before you're born.
Happiness is everywhere around the world,
Always take it with you.

Trevor O'Connor (10)
Thorntree Primary School, Charlton

The Test

I'm sitting looking at this test,
I don't have a clue but I'm trying my best.
Half an hour left to do,
I don't think I'll finish, do you?

Oh no,
There's only twenty minutes to go.
I'm trying not to look,
At the person next to me's book.

I'm thinking really bad,
And now I'm mad.
It's nearly over now,
But I don't know how.

The teacher's coming round to collect the test,
I tried hard, actually my best.
The test is over now, I'm glad,
So now I don't have a reason to still be mad.

Bobby Jennings (10)
Thorntree Primary School, Charlton

How I Feel

Sadness is see-through like small, cold tears.
Love is a rainbow like rainbow balls.
Pain is dark blue like the sky at night-time.
Silence is white like a fluffy cloud on a spring day.
Anger is red like your red heart thumping inside you.
Happiness is bright yellow like the shiny sun.
Jealousy is green like witches' green faces.
But the best one in this poem is love.
Love is a powerful thing, something not to throw away.

Terri Martin (9)
Thorntree Primary School, Charlton

My Demon Family

He's bad, mean and scary,
He's got horns, fangs and is really hairy.
He runs around screaming his head off,
He's so dumb that he thinks I'm a toff.
He scares my mother,
He's my demon brother.

She's always in a bad mood,
She'll eat any food.
She can only shout, not talk,
She is so lazy, she won't walk.
She scares my mother,
She's my demon sister.

I'll break all the mirrors in my house,
I'll squish that annoying little mouse.
I don't keep any friends,
I stole a Mercedes-Benz
I scare my mother,
I'm a demon son.

Jordan Eadon (10)
Thorntree Primary School, Charlton

Colours And Senses

Fear is black like a dark, spooky dungeon.
Anger is red like a devil making soup.
Hate is orange like the fire in your eyes.
Happiness is golden like finding a friend.
Curiosity is green like a big green forest.
And last but certainly not least is love.
Love has no form, no colour, no feel.
It is blank, blank like the mist from a tall mountain.

Seamas Ryan (10)
Thorntree Primary School, Charlton

Colours

Colours are everywhere,
On the carpet,
In the air,
Maybe even in your hair!

Colours are everywhere,
Even if you stop and stare,
What will you see?
Colours everywhere!

Colours are everywhere,
Up and down,
In the fair
And when you win a teddy bear!

Colours are everywhere,
Up the staircase
And in every other place,
Day and night, in the light!

Lauren White (11)
Thorntree Primary School, Charlton

A Sense Poem

Anger is red like boiling lava.
Fear is black like a prison.
Happiness is golden like a bracelet.
Love is pink like a carnation.
Envy is green like the grass.
Curiosity is yellow like the sun.
Pain is purple like a bruise.
Jealousy is blue like the deep blue sea.

Ross-Anthony Monteiro (10)
Thorntree Primary School, Charlton

Sadness

Darkness is swirling around my head,
I am so sad I wish I could die instead.
I know who did it, I wish I did not,
But I don't know if it's making me hot.

I can't pay the ransom to get my girl back,
I wish I had stayed with her by the drying rack.
But with shock and disgust I'm feeling quite weak,
The person who thieved her must be a freak.

I need a miracle to get her back; I went to my friend Hank,
He told me to draw £100,000 out the bank.
I gave the thief the money but he threatened to slaughter,
He threw her out the window. *No!* I wish I had caught her.

Darkness is whirling around my head,
I am so sad I wish I could die instead.
I know who did it, I wish I did not,
But I don't know if it's making me hot.

Callum Jay Grant (11)
Thorntree Primary School, Charlton

Senses You Feel

Fear is black like a wall of charcoal
Love is pink like a beautiful sunset
Hate is grey like a stone crumbling to pieces
Happiness is yellow like a sun on a sunny day
Sadness is blue like a pebble dropping into a lake
Anger is red like blood flowing down a river.

These are all the senses you feel
In all kinds of different ways
But wherever you go they're always there.

Ashleigh Nutton (9)
Thorntree Primary School, Charlton

I'm The Best

I am wonderful because
There's only one of me.

I am made out of
Peaches and cream.

I am the clouds of the
Dream's dream.

I am the cat's whiskers
And the dog's bark.

I am the spaghetti in the
Bolognese sauce.

I am the music on the
Sea and the sand on the
Beach.

And that is *me!*

Tammy Sawyer (10)
Thorntree Primary School, Charlton

Senses You Feel

Anger is red like boiling lava
Grey is grey like a cloudy sky
Love is a rainbow glittering up high
Fear is black like a dark, dark night
Happiness is yellow like daffodils in spring
Sadness is blue like a never-ending ocean
Pain is like a blister on your foot
Jealousy is green like a toad's skin.

Nicholas Bulgen (9)
Thorntree Primary School, Charlton

The Haunted House

The haunted house,
Has every rat and mouse.
The floors creak,
Ghosts and men peek.

Dead girls walk,
Tonight we're eating men and pork.
Blood as wine,
Return to your rooms by nine.

People moving in today,
We've got to make them pay.
Give them a fright,
And a hell of a night.

Screaming so loud,
We ghosts are starting to feel bad.
They're moving out today,
We have definitely made them pay.

Matthew Parsons (11)
Thorntree Primary School, Charlton

The Short Poems

Anger is red like boiling lava.
Hate is orange like hot molten metal.
Fear is black like a witch's cauldron.
Sadness is blue like the deep blue sea.
Happiness is golden like golden daffodils.

Danelle Angus (9)
Thorntree Primary School, Charlton

The Horses

Brown, grey and also bay,
All the different colours that they are.
On the horses
You can ride so far.

Cantering, trotting,
Walking and galloping.
All those different speeds
That you can do.

Jumping, showing,
Racing and games.
All those different things
That you can do.

But all these things
That you can do,
Shouldn't matter to you,
Because you are with the horses.

Hannah West (10)
Thorntree Primary School, Charlton

Senses You Feel

Fear is black like a dark, dark night,
Love is pink like a shining heart,
Hate is grey like a winter storm,
Happiness is yellow like daffodils on a spring day,
Sadness is blue like a rainy day,
Anger is red like an explosion of lava.

Katie Brett (10)
Thorntree Primary School, Charlton

Wintertime

It is wintertime when the snow is falling,
The robins chirping on my window sill,
The babies all happy, gurgling and crawling,
And the owl hibernating in the windmill.

Evergreens growing in my back garden,
Children going down the hill on my sledge,
Ooops, I'm sorry, beg my pardon!
But all the flowers are dead on my ledge.

Santa coming down the chimney,
Reindeers on my rooftop,
My baby sister Kimmy,
Heard Santa's belly go flop.

Outside my door my friends are singing carols,
And I'm drinking my hot choc,
My dad's collecting snow in a barrel,
My biscuits have gone hard like rock.

It's hailing down and pattering on the glass,
I hope Santa comes to knock,
Santa will eat my cookies to the last,
I will wait while I look at the clock.

Winter is fun for everyone,
Snow and frost,
It's cool and if you don't like the sun,
It's perfect for you,
It's perfect for you, it doesn't even cost!

Rachel Diamond (11)
Thorntree Primary School, Charlton

Wintertime Is Here

Winter, when will you come?
It's time to celebrate and have fun,
Christmas is near and not that far,
How about eating a chocolate bar?

Animals are around at this time,
How about a nice lemon and lime?
People are having so much fun,
If you're cold - how about a run?

Birds are in the sky flying,
While people are buying,
Sliding down in the sledge,
Be careful not to hit a ledge!

Birds are in migration,
While animals are in hibernation,
People are skating on ice,
Being friendly and nice.

It's time to have Christmas lights,
How about a snowball fight?
Build a snowman big as you can!
Have a Christmas dinner at your nan's!

Snow is coming down on the ground,
Santa is very big and very round!
Jesus was born on Christmas Day,
There in Bethlehem where he lay.

Vishal Koria (10)
Thorntree Primary School, Charlton

What Hairstyle Should I Wear Today?

What hairstyle should I wear today?
Long, short or silky flowing,
Black, brown or golden glowing,
White, blonde or something showing?
What hairstyle should I wear today?

What hairstyle should I wear today?
Wild, calm or frizzy curls,
Straight, bright or twisty twirls,
Hairy, scary or bizarre whirls?
What hairstyle should I wear today?

What hairstyle should I wear today?
Streaks, plain or in-between?
Sparkly, shiny, I'm really keen,
To find a hairstyle just for me.
What hairstyle should I wear today?

Ndidi Aliago (10)
Thorntree Primary School, Charlton

Hospital

I woke up this morning,
Wondering where I was,
I saw two of everything,
In fact I saw two nurses coming towards me.

I was scared.

I looked beside me, there was Mum,
Drinking lots of gin and rum,
She looked worried,
So was I,
I felt like I was going to cry.

I asked my mum what was going on,
She explained then sang a song,
I felt better after a while,
So I decided to give her a smile.

Ashleigh Ford (10)
Thorntree Primary School, Charlton

The Crazy Ark

The animals went in two by two,
The elephant and the kangaroo.
The lion, the tiger, the cat and the dog,
The mouse, the gorilla, the rat and the frog.
But they could only find one dinosaur,
This is why they aren't around anymore.

The animals went in two by two,
The kiwi and the pygmy shrew,
The spider, the beetle, the monkey and hog,
The big alligator that looks like a log.
But they could only find one Nessie,
This is why they are really messy.

Heather Barrett (10)
Thorntree Primary School, Charlton

The Gingerbread Man

The gingerbread man once he was fully baked,
Jumped out of the oven where he faked,
To be unalive, tasty and tan,
Until he was spotted, then he got up and ran.
Running, running, with a cheesy grin,
Tip-tap, tip-tap, looks small like a pin,
Darting and parting away from all behind,
The old lady, the old man and a cow in a line.
A bunch of children, a cat and a dog chased him too,
But then the dog stopped, he needed to use the loo.
Darting and parting from all behind,
Stopping only to see a fox looking not so kind.
He was searching, searching for a place to hide,
Said the fox, 'There's a lake. Do you want a ride?'
'OK,' said the gingerbread man, 'you mean no harm.'
But when they got over he had lost more than just his arm!

Jasmine Timbres (11)
Walnut Tree Walk Primary School, Lambeth

Lion

The king of the jungle
A loud roarer
A big scratcher
A bird eater.

A soft creature
A water drinker
A jungle leader
A meat eater.

A good leaper
A tree sleeper
A long-tailed creature
A golden colour.

A big creature
A long-clawed creature
A hairy creature
A serious fighter.

Nicole Lightfoot (9)
Walnut Tree Walk Primary School, Lambeth

Parrot

A good speaker
A worm eater
A good drinker
A good blinker

A shoulder sitter
A fruit lover
A talking mimer
A fantastic pecker.

Devontaê Thomas (8)
Walnut Tree Walk Primary School, Lambeth

Little Red Riding Hood

Time to go to Grandma's,
She's very, very sick,
Here is the basket,
Skip along quick.

Skip, skip, skip along,
Make sure you stay on the path,
Look at the deep, dark, spooky woods,
Stick out your arm and the wolf will have half!

The woods have pretty flowers,
I think I'll go in,
I'm nearly at Grandma's house,
The sky is starting to dim.

I've reached her house,
Skip along through the door,
Into her bedroom,
She's changed a lot from before.

Wow, what big eyes you have!
Wow, what a big bum you've got!
Wow, what a big mouth you have!
All the better to eat your body - the whole lot!

There's a big set of sharp teeth,
Getting ready to eat me,
Suddenly someone bursts in through the door,
Yeah, my life is to be.

A man comes and saves my grandma,
He cuts open the wolf's belly,
I'm so happy to be safe,
I can go home and watch telly.

It's a joyful, happy ending,
The big bad wolf is gone!

Rosa Lynch-Northover (11)
Walnut Tree Walk Primary School, Lambeth

Dentist

A teeth fixer
A hole driller
A teeth replacer
A braces implanter

A child's fear
A sticker giver
A teeth brusher
A busy worker

A teeth checker
A teeth helper
A special water drinker
A tool user

A receptionist spare worker
A drill user
A teeth puller
A little mirror user

A toothbrush giver
A helper
A chair controller
An appointment checker.

Lewis Ozanne-Martin (9)
Walnut Tree Walk Primary School, Lambeth

The Writer Of This Poem

(Based on 'The Writer of this Poem' by Roger McGough)

The writer of this poem
Is neater than the Queen
As quiet as the sea
As sweet as a tambourine
As friendly as can be
As pretty as a ballerina.

Faiza Mirza (10)
West Hill Primary School, Wandsworth

I Remember, Remember

I remember, remember the fifth of November
When my grandpa died

My heart was big as the universe
Now it's as small as a crumb

I remember, remember the ice cream after dinner
'Mum, dessert, oh . . . no more!'

I remember, remember the jokes and the tickles
He-he-he, no more laughter!

I remember, remember I was as bright as the sun
Now I'm deep, deep dark

I remember, remember the bony knee
And the squeezes he gave me

I remember my grandpa.

Jodie Bateman (9)
West Hill Primary School, Wandsworth

Love Is . . .

Love is the scent of the reddest rose petal
Dipped in clear, clean spring water from a fairyland fountain.
Love is the silky touch of leather
Made into new, shiny, black school shoes.
Love is the scaly body of the shiny, colourful rainbowfish
In the deep blue ocean.
Love is the taste of a cherry made in sweet Heaven by angels
In the gentle blue sky up so high.
Love is the care from your mum, dad, sister and brother
That is kept in your heart forever.

Arjona Hoxha (7)
West Hill Primary School, Wandsworth

Silence

A stranger came this morning
Took me to a world,
A world of silence.

He took my voice,
And put it in a bag,
And left me,
In this other world.

As in silence,
Without the crunching of the toast,
And ticking of the clock.
I stayed in silence.

As time goes on without hearing,
The world has stopped,
I thought I'd dream,
But I did not.

As I go deaf,
My life has changed.
I wonder would my life change any more?

Kubra Sarigul (10)
West Hill Primary School, Wandsworth

Love Is . . .

Love is the sweet, fresh smell of the morning sunshine
When I get out of my cosy bed.
Love is the delicious, splendid taste of cold, soft rice pudding
When I am eating it all up.
Love is when people put their past behind them
And make best friends.
Love is what you can do for people who you don't even know
And who are very sick and in serious trouble.
Love is the sweet, tender care of a child with his parents
Who love him very much.

Michael Adjenim-Boateng (8)
West Hill Primary School, Wandsworth

Have You Ever Seen A . . . ?

Have you ever seen a dog?
Hole-maker,
Bone-catcher,
Cat-hunter,
Meat-smeller,
Stick-fetcher.

Have you ever seen a cat?
Dog-hater,
Soft-stroker,
Fish-lover,
Bird-catcher.

Have you ever seen a dolphin?
Jump-lover,
People-listener,
Fish-eater,
Fast-swimmer.

Mustafa Sarigul (9)
West Hill Primary School, Wandsworth

Love Is . . .

Love is the strong smell of the freshly cut green grass
With lots of colourful flowers growing in it.
Love is seeing your mum and dad
When you wake up in the morning.
Love is the sound of the birds singing in the morning
When the sun rises.
Love is the distant sound of the ice cream van
As you lay on the soft, smooth sand.
Love is the touch of a smooth, soft, gentle dolphin.

Rebekah Upfold (8)
West Hill Primary School, Wandsworth

Love Is . . .

Love is the taste of sweet, fresh, juicy strawberries
With puddles of silky soft cream.
Love is the sound of juice pouring out of a tropical fruit
As it's being squeezed.
Love is the sequins floating on the clean, blue, fresh water
Making them shine in the blue sky.
Love is the touching of a colourful singing of a fluffy flamingo bird.
Love is the special day for your mum.
Sing your mum songs to make her happy
Because it's Valentine's Day.

Taylor Wynne-Sutton (8)
West Hill Primary School, Wandsworth

Love Is . . .

Love is the taste of warm, delicious, chocolate custard
And chocolate cake.
Love is the sound of the beautiful, colourful, singing birds
In summer.
Love is the smell of the sweet, grassy, sunny spring.
Love is the feel of soft, little, new leaves in springtime.
Love is the grass and flowers that grow in the summertime.

Michael O'Toole (8)
West Hill Primary School, Wandsworth

Love Is . . .

Love is when I smell the sweet cranberry juice when it is ice-cold.
Love is the sweet, juicy, red taste of strawberries
And lots of soft cream.
Love is when I can feel warm inside me and wherever I go
Because my mum's love keeps me safe.
Love is when I can spend lots of time with my mum.
Love is the sweet, fresh smell of the air when it is hot outside.

Paige Springer (8)
West Hill Primary School, Wandsworth

Love Is . . .

Love is the sweet smell of flowers.
Love is the sweet sound of the sea crashing on the rocks.
Love is the nice air, the great smell of the sea.
Love is hearing my mum's heartbeat.
Love is the bell ringing.
Love is the sweet smell of ice cream.
Love is the perfume on your mum's chest
When you give her a hug.
Love is the sweet touch of berries.
Love is the soft strawberries.

Mario Bennett (7)
West Hill Primary School, Wandsworth

Love Is . . .

Love is the sweet whistling birds on a summer morning.
Love is the sweet smell of cut oranges and apples on a plate.
Love is a touch of the juicy red strawberries growing on a bush.
Love is the sweet taste of purple juicy grapes
When they pop in your mouth.
Love is the sweet scent of the tall, colourful, fresh grass
Swishing in the breeze.

Melissa Peterson (8)
West Hill Primary School, Wandsworth

Love Is . . .

Love is the warm heart of God when I am asleep.
Love is the sweet smell of red roses when I sniff them.
Love is the warm sunshine over me when I am at the beach.
Love is the soft, creamy, warm taste of custard.
Love is the sound of birds singing softly in the garden.

Kayla Collett (7)
West Hill Primary School, Wandsworth

Quiet

It is so quiet I can hear
The candles whispering to one another.
It is so quiet I can hear
The windowpane sigh as it basks in the sun.
It is so quiet I can hear
The pages moan with relief as the paper turns.
It is so quiet I can hear
The floorboards giggle as we tickle them with our toes.
It is so quiet I can hear
The page reading as we write words.
It is so quiet I can hear
The carpet cry, 'Ouch!' as the pin drops.
It is so quiet I can hear
A single heartbeat and my body singing along.

Carly Abdul Dyges (11)
West Hill Primary School, Wandsworth

Love Is . . .

Love is the taste of pink, gorgeous strawberry milkshake
On a summer's day.
Love is the scent of still, sweet, summer, fresh flowers
On a very special day.
Love is the sound of the gold church bells ringing
When someone is getting married on a summer's day.
Love is the touch of a shiny, cute face of a newborn baby
In a noisy hospital on a spring day.
Love is the sight of a cute, funny, fast kitten
Playing around in the garden on a summer's day.

Natalie Rayworth (7)
West Hill Primary School, Wandsworth

Have You Ever Seen A . . . ?

Have you ever seen a dolphin?
Water-splasher,
Tail-flicker,
Fish-chaser,
Good-diver.

Have you ever seen a pig?
Tail-curler,
Loud-grunter,
Mud-roller,
Cabbage-smeller.

Have you ever seen a butterfly?
Wing-flapper,
Fast-flyer,
Nectar-collector,
Colour-spreader.

Ishan Guthrie-Miller (8)
West Hill Primary School, Wandsworth

Love Is . . .

Love is the taste of the fresh, crunchy, juicy, green apple
In the first two bites.
Love is the smell of the fresh, green trees swaying
In the spring breeze.
Love is the sound of the blue, sweet, tweeting birds
In the afternoon.
Love is the touch of a dog's warm belly next to the fire.
Love is looking a the bright, colourful flowers
In the summer morning.

Kayla Bishop (7)
West Hill Primary School, Wandsworth

Have You Ever Seen A . . . ?

Have you ever seen a monkey?
Tail-swisher,
High-jumper,
Tree-swinger,
Cheeky-thinker.

Have you ever seen a butterfly?
Fast-flyer,
Nectar-collector
Wing-flapper,
Colourful-creature.

Have you ever seen a snake?
Blood-sucker,
Slimy-slitherer,
Blood-spitter,
Human-strangler,
Mouse-hunter.

Have you ever seen a spider?
Fast-runner,
Hairy-walker,
Blood-sucker,
High-jumper.

Alia Ahmad (8)
West Hill Primary School, Wandsworth

Love Is . . .

Love is the taste of sweet red strawberries.
Love is the scent of the reddest rose petal on a summer day.
Love is the feel of the white fluffy swan sitting by the lake.
Love is the sweet singing of the fairies up in the bright blue sky.
Love is the sight of the bright, blue, fresh, shiny river.

Maleeha Abdullah (8)
West Hill Primary School, Wandsworth

My Deep Treasures

I put on goggles ready to dive
Jump, *splish, splash, splosh.*

When I move so slow, so steady
I feel like I'm in a ball pool,
So slow, so steady.

I find a shell where there are pearls,
So shiny, so round,
The best pearls in the world.

Fishes swimming differently,
Beautiful colours gleaming so bright.

I see a fish glow like glitter,
I see a shark swim so fine,
I see an octopus helping the fish.

I get out of the floatation tank,
I think of the beautiful underworld.

Omara Kamran (10)
West Hill Primary School, Wandsworth

Love Is . . .

Love is the taste of round, vibrant, spring fresh cherries.
Love is fresh as the sweet, cold, see-through water
Flowing down the silky rocks.
Love is the smell of singing, silky, harmonising birds
With happy, joyful souls.
Love is the smell of fresh ice cream and strawberries
With oodles of silky flowing cream.
Love is the taste of delicious, hot, boiling, spicy peppers.

Charlotte Clarke (7)
West Hill Primary School, Wandsworth

Have You Ever Seen A . . . ?

Have you ever seen a dog?
Meat-lover,
Treat-taker,
Person-protector,
Playful-jumper.

Have you ever seen a cat?
Soft-scratcher,
Loud-purrer,
Stroke-lover,
Tree-climber.

Have you ever seen an elephant?
Slow-plodder,
Water-spouter,
Grey-drinker,
Footstep-maker.

Have you ever seen a spider?
Little-crawler,
Drain-lover,
Web-weaver,
Scary-treader.

Steven Wilson-Adams (8)
West Hill Primary School, Wandsworth

My Fish

In my fish tank it is still as a rock.
There's no more watching the fish.
No more humming of the motor.
Now it's peaceful, no more fish catching each other.
Now it's just an empty tank.

Ali Mir (9)
West Hill Primary School, Wandsworth

Have You Ever Seen A . . . ?

Have you ever seen a cat?
Proud-purrer,
Fish-lover,
Dog-hater,
Milk-drinker.

Have you ever seen a dog?
Cat-hater,
Meat-lover,
Loud-barker,
Danger-sensor.

Have you ever seen a horse?
Fast-galloper,
Mane-waver,
Race-winner,
Carrot-lover.

Have you ever seen a fish?
Fast-swimmer,
Seaweed-eater,
Tail-waver,
Shark's-dinner.

Lydia Iwheta (9)
West Hill Primary School, Wandsworth

The Sea

The sea is a ferocious beast
Who runs back and forth
With his roar so loud
He likes to take victims with him
And drag them deep in his home
Taking bodies with him
And spit the ruins onto different lands.

Peter Kitakufe (11)
West Hill Primary School, Wandsworth

Have You Ever Seen A . . . ?

Have you ever seen a guinea pig?
Cute-creature,
Soft-scuttler,
Silly-squeaker,
Food-finder.

Have you ever seen a rabbit?
Hairy-hopper,
Bunny-bouncer,
Powder puff-pounder,
Long jump-lover.

Have you ever seen a mouse?
Scared-skipper,
Naughty-nibbler,
Cheesy-chomper,
Cheeky-chewer.

Have you ever seen a cat?
Wool-wanter,
Skin-scratcher,
Claw-clinger,
Fur-fluffer.

Have you ever seen a penguin?
Belly-bouncer,
Super-slider,
Jolly-jumper,
Snow-skidder.

Matilda Woollen (8)
West Hill Primary School, Wandsworth

Have You Ever Seen A . . . ?

Have you ever seen a lion?
Loud-roarer,
Vicious-attacker,
Hairy-maneater,
Mane-shaker.

Have you ever seen a bee?
Busy-buzzer,
Honey-maker,
Pollen-collector,
Angry-stinger.

Have you ever seen a kangaroo?
High-hopper,
Pouch-hugger,
Fast-runner,
Plant-eater.

Have you ever seen a cat?
Loud-purrer,
Mouse-catcher,
Tail-swisher,
Eye-flasher.

Have you ever seen a snake?
Sly-slitherer,
Egg-swallower,
Venom-spitter,
Human-strangler.

Charlie Bishop (8)
West Hill Primary School, Wandsworth

Have You Ever Seen A . . . ?

Have you ever seen a cat?
Cute-cuddler,
Proud-stroller,
Food-cruncher,
Loud-purrer.

Have you ever seen a butterfly?
Silent-flyer,
Colourful-flutterer,
Delicate-soarer,
Nectar-gatherer.

Have you ever seen a dolphin?
Water-splasher,
Long-jumper,
Shiny-swimmer,
Hoop-leaper.

Have you ever seen a penguin?
White-waddler,
Beak-snapper,
Belly-tapper,
Tummy-slider.

Have you ever seen a bunny?
Cuddly-skipper,
Hairy-hopper,
Jolly-jumper,
Carrot-cruncher.

Have you ever seen a pig?
Snout-snorter,
Mud-roller,
Meat-eater,
Pink-porker.

Murwarid Laly (9)
West Hill Primary School, Wandsworth

Have You Ever Seen A . . . ?

Have you ever seen a kitten?
Silent-purrer,
Cute-cuddler,
Fish-eater,
Cuddly-creature.

Have you ever seen a butterfly?
Silent-flyer,
Colourful-winger,
Tiny-eyed,
And the smallest creature.

Have you ever seen a dolphin?
Long-beaker,
Cute-cuddler,
Water-splasher,
Deep-diver.

Have you ever seen a pig?
Loud-snorer,
Big-eater,
Pork-chopper,
Pink-piggy.

Have you ever seen a kangaroo?
High-jumper,
Goo-googler,
Pouch-poucher,
Food-hunter.

Angel Bascom (8)
West Hill Primary School, Wandsworth

The Clouds

The clouds are like white, fluffy sheep,
In a meadowy field,
Who are hopping around,
In very small leaps.

The clouds are like puffy candyfloss,
Which are very nice and sweet,
And fill the children with happiness and joy,
And they'd even sing and tweet.

The clouds are like a bag of cotton wool,
That are spread around the sky,
And in the night they fade away,
As they lay down and hide.

Well, all I want to say is,
That if there wasn't the sky,
There wouldn't be any clouds,
And I think I'd probably start to cry.

Hajra Bibi Islam (10)
West Hill Primary School, Wandsworth

The Sea

The sea is a vicious beast
He growls and makes a wave
He clashes his teeth and makes earthquakes
He chews on the rubbish you throw
Keeps it down below
Sinks ships like the Titanic!

Luka Radic (11)
West Hill Primary School, Wandsworth

The Clouds

The clouds are like cotton wool
On a blue piece of paper.

The clouds are like fluffy sheep
Moving around happily.

The clouds are like candyfloss
That is tasty and sweet.

The clouds are like a white dress
Which is cute and puffy.

The clouds are like a soft, flat area
Which will always be safe.

The clouds are like a white Afro
Which is very bouncy.

The clouds are like a white bush
That isn't prickly.

The clouds are kind and belong to the sky
Which makes everyone happy and full of joy.

James Paul Nottage (10)
West Hill Primary School, Wandsworth

Hate

Dark, black and desolate
Bitter but tasteless
Fire, smoke and brimstone
A black river of dead souls
Loud thoughts *booming*
Of hatred and jealousy
Cold and empty
Stark.

Claire Lawton (11)
West Hill Primary School, Wandsworth

If Only I Could Change The Past

If only I could change the past
I would stop the war happening and the killing.
I would, I would completely change the past forever.
If I could change the past
I would stop people dying
And there would be more surviving and more people living.
That would be fine.
I would, I would change the past.
If I could change the past
I would stop people being nasty
And people would be so very happy,
Not sad, just happy.
I would, I would change the past forever.
And if I could go very, very, very far
I could go into the past
I would be able to go and see my granny and grandad
And hug them and wouldn't leave them
So I could see them before they died
And they'd still be alive.
And most of all I would stop my auntie dying
And make her see what's wrong with herself
So she wouldn't die and the whole of my family would be happy
And she'd still be alive.
I miss her so much,
If only I could change the past.
If only . . . I wish!

Agnes Tedman (9)
West Hill Primary School, Wandsworth

The Funfair

Have you ever been to a funfair?
Well, let me tell you about it.
People are
Screaming, shouting
Yelling, shivering
Running, shrieking
That's what people do at the funfair.

Have you ever been on a ride that twists you upside down?
Well, let me tell you about it.
It goes
Up and down
Side to side
Spinning around
Spin, spin, spin, spin.
That's how a ride twists you upside down.

Have you ever been to a funfair where people eat?
Well, let me tell you about it.
They are
Munching,
Swallowing,
Drinking.
That's what happens at the funfair.

Hemanth Jois (10)
West Hill Primary School, Wandsworth

Have You Ever Seen A . . . ?

Have you ever seen a dog?
Big-barker,
Fast-runner,
Treat-eater,
Funny-player.

Have you ever seen a horse?
Fast-galloper,
Hay-eater,
Lazy-sleeper,
Slow-walker.

Have you ever seen a bird?
Fast-flier,
Egg-layer,
Quick-catcher,
Worm-eater.

Kieran Holligan (8)
West Hill Primary School, Wandsworth

Love And Hate

This is what I think of love:
Love is a pink rose,
Love is sweet candyfloss,
Love smells like my morning laundry,
Love looks like a heart pumping,
Love sounds like wedding bells in the summer,
Love feels like a duckling being born.

This is what I think of hate:
Hate is a black cave,
Hate is a sour sweet you can never get the sourness out of,
Hate is a leaf that can't fall off a tree,
Hate is the Devil being born.

Jessica Cremin (11)
West Hill Primary School, Wandsworth

Untitled

(Based on 'The Sound Collector' by Roger McGough)

'A stranger called this morning,
Dressed all in black and grey,
Put all the sounds into a bag
And carried them away.'

The switching of the light,
The whooshing of the kite,
The crying of the baby,
The chattering of the ladies.

The ticking of the clock,
The smashing of the rocks,
The beating of the heart,
The munching of jam tarts.

This stranger called this morning
Dressed all in black and grey
Without these sounds,
Life will never be the same.

Zeeshan Ahmad (10)
West Hill Primary School, Wandsworth

My Kitten

Big, cuddly,
Hungry for food,
Nice brown eyes,
Carpet scratcher,
My best friend.

Mikyila Leonard (8)
West Hill Primary School, Wandsworth